The Preposterous Adventures of Swimmer

Westminster Press Books
by Alexander Key

THE
PREPOSTEROUS
ADVENTURES
OF SWIMMER

by

Alexander Key

THE WESTMINSTER PRESS
PHILADELPHIA

PUBLISHED BY THE WESTMINSTER PRESS®
PHILADELPHIA, PENNSYLVANIA

PRINTED IN THE UNITED STATES OF AMERICA

Library of Congress Cataloging in Publication Data

Key, Alexander.
  The preposterous adventures of Swimmer.

  SUMMARY: A talking river otter escapes from
captivity, experiences perilous adventures with some
cruel humans, and resolves the problems of various
troubled people and animals.
  [1. Otters—Stories] I. Title.
PZ7.K51Pr   [Fic]   73–7945
ISBN 0–664–32537–8

Contents

To a certain knowing otter
    I met on a stream one day.
May his tribe increase.

1

He Opens a Cage

Swimmer's first escape was a tricky bit of business that required the most of his cleverness and stealth. It involved unlatching the iron gate to his pen, opening the laboratory door and the one to the hall, then slipping all the way through Dr. Hoffman's sumptuous town house to the front entrance, which had two locks.

The most delicate part of the operation, which Swimmer considered great fun, was stealing past the two guardian bulldogs who had no use whatever for an educated otter with a silver bell around his neck. The bell was a tinkling nuisance he had been unable to get rid of, so he held it between his teeth until he had fiddled with the locks and was safely outside.

On the sidewalk Swimmer froze, shocked by the unexpected rush of midnight traffic. Dogs and doors he could deal with, but the horror of man's traffic was something else. Finally, seeing his chance, he streaked across the avenue and managed to make it unharmed to the park on the other side.

A sort of creek, he knew, wound through the park and opened into a canal not far away. Somewhere in the smoggy distance the canal emptied into a river. Up that river, surely, lay wildness and freedom.

As he slid eagerly down to the creek, Swimmer had a momentary vision of the sparkling stream he had played in as a pup. It was a delightful place—full of crawfish and trout, and with hundreds of little waterfalls and pools to explore. He and his family had spent a wonderful summer in it before being captured.

The pleasant vision instantly dissolved as the murky creek closed over him. He came up snorting in disgust. The water, he thought, was enough to make a mud turtle gag.

Determinedly, though, he sped forward in the direction of the canal. It couldn't possibly be much worse there than here. If he could stand it till he reached the river, he'd soon be out of man's world forever.

The canal gave him another shock, but it was the reeking river that stopped him. The river was a horror.

So by daybreak Swimmer was back at his prison. There was nothing else to do, unless he wanted to tackle the immensity of the city on foot, facing a nightmare of traffic.

Since it was impossible to enter the house the way he had left it, he went around to the service entrance and waited for the arrival of Clarence, the black caretaker.

At the sight of Swimmer, Clarence's long jaw sagged. "Swat me down!" he muttered. "Who let you out?"

"Nobody," Swimmer said irritably, in the voice of an exasperated gnome. He was in a high state of disgust, as well as a little sick at his stomach. "Stop staring like a gloop and let me in."

It was the first time he had ever spoken directly to anyone, though he had often used his voice to play jokes on Miss Primm, his teacher in the lab.

Clarence swallowed, clearly jolted. He was very lean and had a thin, shrewd face. Suddenly he slapped his knee and began to laugh. "So it's you that's been saying 'Hi, dovey!' to Miss Primm and kidding her along! And we thought it was the mynah bird. I should have *known* you could talk."

Swimmer grunted. He had never thought very highly of the human voice. There were more pleasant sounds. "I'm not proud of it. Are you going to tell Doc about me?"

"Of course not! He wouldn't believe it, anyway. And don't call me a gloop. I'm your friend."

"Honest?"

"Honest, cross my heart," Clarence told him solemnly.

Swimmer studied him a moment. Of all the humans he had come to know since his capture, he liked Clarence best. Which wasn't saying much, of course, for there wasn't much you could say about the whole human tribe. But at least Clarence had always been good to him, and he was not a pompous old goat like Doc.

"Clarence," he said slowly, "would you help me escape?"

"Escape? Hey, what kind of talk is this? Were you trying to run away this morning?"

"I'll tell you when I've had some breakfast. Let's go inside before somebody sees us."

The lab was a separate wing of the house where the much-talked-about Dr. Rufus Hoffman was studying animal intelligence. It seemed to Swimmer that Miss Primm, Clarence, and the various secretaries did all the work and studying while Dr. Hoffman, when he was not away lecturing, merely strode about majestically, playing the role of God. Once there had been more than a dozen captive creatures in the place, including three other otters in the enclosure with the otter pool. Now the lab housed only a white mouse, a black mynah bird, and himself.

As he slid into the pool to erase the smells he had acquired during the night, the white mouse sent forth a thought of inquiry: *How did you find the world outside?*

It stinks, Swimmer told him.

I knew it was better here, the mouse replied. *You are safe and warm, and there is plenty of food. What more do you want?*

You wouldn't know. You were born here.

The mynah bird sent a thought: *I know. I remember the great forest where I was born. But I can only dream.* Aloud, in a voice like a bell, he called, "Another day, another dollar. Oh, what a wonderful life!"

Swimmer sniffed uncertainly at a dish of shrimp Clarence placed before him and wondered what Dr. Hoffman would think if he were told of the silent conversations that went on among the prisoners. Old Doc probably wouldn't believe it. But Clarence would. Clarence was one of those very few humans who could sometimes feel things that couldn't be seen or heard.

"Now, let's get this straight," Clarence was saying. "You really were trying to run away, eh?"

"I had it in mind," Swimmer admitted.

"Then what happened that made you come back?"

When he had explained to Clarence about the river, the black man said, "You've been here nearly three years. Why didn't you try running away before?"

"Because I wasn't ready. I was only a pup when I came here, and that's a crazy world out there. What chance would I have had?"

"And now you think you're ready?"

"I've been ready," Swimmer acknowledged sourly. "I've had it to the teeth with education. *Your* kind, I mean. And I don't like these shrimp. They stink."

"But they're the best shrimp money can buy!" Clarence protested.

"I know it. I don't blame you. It's the way things are.

If you'd ever tasted a crawfish right out of a high-country pool . . ."

Clarence tugged thoughtfully at his jaw. "I see what you mean, Swimmer. And you think it's better where you came from?"

"Of course it's better!"

"And you want me to help you escape?"

"That's the idea. Will you?"

Clarence slowly shook his head. "No. I think that would be wrong."

Swimmer kicked over the dish of shrimp. "You said you were my friend! What's wrong about helping me?"

"It's like this," Clarence began patiently. "You're no more fitted to go back and live where you came from than I am to go to Africa and live off monkey meat, like my people once did. You see? Nature would kill us. We're soft and weak. We're *civilized*. Anyone as smart as you—"

They were interrupted by the opening of the laboratory door and Miss Primm's forcibly cheery greeting, "Good morning, all. How are we this morning?"

Clarence said, " 'Morning, miss," and the mynah bird, in a perfect imitation of Swimmer's gnomelike voice, called, "Hi, dovey!"

Miss Primm gave a little sniff, then smiled and took her seat at the desk facing the otter pool.

"Swimmer," she began brightly, "I've just had the most exciting talk with Dr. Hoffman. We're to appear at two big lectures next week—Washington and Nashville. Isn't that wonderful? So we must work very, very hard to improve our spelling. We wouldn't want to shame the doctor before all those important people, would we?"

Swimmer almost said Phooey, but controlled himself and scrambled over to an apparatus with a keyboard like a giant typewriter. Whenever he pressed a key, a large tab with the same letter on it would flip up on the board behind him.

Quickly he tapped out: N-O S-C-H-O-L T-O-D-A-Y. H-A-D B-A-D N-I-T-E. F-E-E-L L-O-W-S-Y.

Without another glance at her, he crawled into his concrete den and curled up to sleep. Maybe his spelling wasn't so hot, but there wasn't a thing wrong with his geography. He knew exactly where Nashville was. To reach it from Washington, Clarence would have to drive their van across the high country where he had lived as a pup.

The very thought of it sent an excited tingling through Swimmer.

Whenever Swimmer was scheduled to appear at one of the great Dr. Hoffman's lectures, he and Clarence would travel in the van, which also carried the big apparatus with the keyboard and the lettered tabs. The doctor usually went in his limousine, and Swimmer saw little of him until it was time to begin answering questions at the keyboard.

Though the doctor treated him like a laboratory creation, Swimmer often found it great fun to be in front of an audience, the center of attention. It was that way in Washington. He was an immediate hit with the bigwigs, who soon began asking questions of their own.

"Swimmer," said a famous senator, "what do you think of people?"

He tapped out: N-O-T H-A-F A-S M-U-C-H A-S T-H-E-Y T-H-I-N-K O-F T-H-E-M-S-E-L-V-E-S.

Another asked, "What is your opinion of money?"

V-E-R-Y L-O-W, he replied. Y-O-U O-U-G-H-T-A G-E-T R-I-D O-F I-T.

"Swimmer, do you believe in God?"

W-H-O E-L-S-E C-O-U-L-D H-A-V-E C-R-E-A-T-E-D A-N O-T-T-E-R?

"Swimmer, how do you feel about your benefactor, Dr. Hoffman?"

H-E-S N-O B-E-N-N-Y F-A-C-T-O-R. H-E-S A-N O-L-D F-R-A-W-D.

The audience was still laughing when a uniformed Clarence hauled him off the stage and locked him in his cage in the van.

"You ought to be ashamed of yourself," said Clarence. "You had no right to say such a thing about Doc in front of all those people."

"Why not? That's how I feel."

"But you didn't have to say it. He's been good to you. You have a fine home, the best food—"

"Aw, fiffle! I'm nothing but a trained slave, and you know it. He bought me and my sister from that dirty trapper just to experiment with, and instead of trying to help her when she got sick, he told the vet to get rid of her. He was through with her anyway—"

"Now, Swimmer," Clarence interrupted. "I've explained how it was. She had to be taken out of the pen to protect the rest of you. But it was too late. All of you got sick. It's too bad the others died, but . . ."

"Go 'way," Swimmer muttered. "I hate you. I hate your whole stinking tribe."

For a little while, remembering his mother, whom the trapper had killed, and playful little Sprite, his sister, he really did hate the entire human race. What Clarence did not suspect was that Swimmer could always tell how people felt toward him, and usually what they were thinking. So could the white mouse and the mynah bird and every other creature he had met except man. Dr. Hoffman's true feelings had never been hidden from them.

Since Clarence liked to drive at night, the van was headed west for Nashville as soon as the keyboard-and-tabs machine was loaded. With the van in motion, Swimmer's mood changed. Immediately he turned to a lower corner of the cage and began digging at the fastenings.

Three of the fastenings were clinched nails that held the heavy wire to the frame. By turning the bent nails a little more, the wire could be loosened. It ought to give plenty of space for four and a half feet of overly educated otter to squirm through.

Sometime after midnight Clarence halted near an all-night restaurant. "I'm going in for coffee, Swimmer. Can I bring you anything?"

Swimmer was not hungry, but he figured he ought to eat all he could while he had the chance. "How about some fish?"

He was surprised and momentarily delighted when Clarence brought him a mountain trout only a few hours out of the hatchery. "Hey, let me sit up front with you and eat it," he begged. "I can't see the country stuck back here."

Clarence sighed. "Sorry, old pal. You're to stay in the cage, and I'm to keep it and the van locked at all times. Those are Doc's orders. And don't get any bright ideas about running away. Just remember you're civilized. You belong with Doc."

"Aw, fiffle! Then how about taking off this crazy bell for a while? I'm nearly out of my ratted mind with it."

"You never complained about the bell before."

"I'm complaining about it now! All it does is tinkle, tinkle, tinkle—"

"Swimmer, you know I can't remove the bell without ruining the harness. That's silver chain."

His spirits fell as the van got under way again. The bell was a danger. How he was going to get rid of it he didn't know, but first he had to break out of the cage, and the fastenings were giving him trouble. As he struggled with them

14

he heard thunder overhead, then the sudden slash of rain. A strange uneasiness came over him.

The rain increased and became a steady downpour as the van wound upward into higher country. It was spring, and through a partially open window came the rich smells of a blossoming earth and occasionally the loved sound of rushing waters. Swimmer was aware of these, but he was robbed of all joy by a growing apprehension. Something was wrong. He forgot the fish entirely.

Suddenly he turned from the fastenings and examined the cage door, shaking it in the hope that the lock hadn't caught. But the lock was secure, and the key was in Clarence's pocket.

The feeling of wrongness grew. Swimmer whirled back to the fastenings, and the van shook as the night seemed to explode with swirling wind and rain. All at once, in a sureness of danger closing upon them, he hurled himself against the wire and cried shrilly, "Stop, Clarence! Stop! Stop the van!"

The loosened wire gave under his frenzy of motion, and he burst out of the cage like a ball, spun about, and leaped forward to the driver's seat.

A startled Clarence had time only to gasp, and instinctively he pressed the brake. That alone saved them. A second later and a couple of feet beyond, the van would have been crushed by the tons of rock that came sliding down the high slope on the right. Clarence jerked the wheel, and the van skidded on the wet paving and turned completely around. There was a moment when the swinging headlights edged a plunging boulder and a falling tree, then the van struck the guardrail on the other side of the road and stopped abruptly. He sat clutching the wheel, dazed.

"Are—are you all right, Clarence?" Swimmer said worriedly.

15

"I—I think so. Lordy, what a close one!" Suddenly Clarence sat up. "Hey—what—how—how did you know something was going to happen?"

"I just knew." Swimmer could have told him that even a one-eyed newt would have felt the approach of danger.

"How did you get out of your cage?"

"I just got out. I had to. This is good-by, Clarence. I'm leaving."

Even as he spoke, Swimmer was hurrying to the rear door of the van. It was locked, but he knew that from inside the van only a quick upward jerk of the handle was needed to release the lock, and the door would swing open.

"No!" Clarence cried, lurching to his feet. "No! You can't do that! Swimmer, listen to me. You're not wild anymore. You'll die out there. Honest—"

Swimmer had already grasped the handle. He threw his weight against it. There was a click, and the door swung open a few inches into the wind. Instantly he sprang for the ground several feet away.

But a devil rode the wind that night. Halfway through the opening Swimmer felt the sudden shift and tried to twist away. He did not quite make it. The door slammed against a leg and held him dangling a moment as pain shot through the leg. When he dropped to the ground the leg was numb.

For uncertain seconds he crouched beside the van, shocked and trembling. Then he became aware of the sound and scent of the stream somewhere beyond the guardrail. Slowly, almost fearfully, he began limping through the blackness toward it.

16

2

He Follows a Trail

The creek was far down a rocky slope, and it was high and roaring from the spring rains. In the mountain dark, with one leg useless, Swimmer reached it only with the greatest difficulty.

Before his capture he would have plunged happily into the wildest water and found it great sport to battle the current. But now, even though he couldn't see the stream, its very thunder terrified him. He sank down in the brush near the water, shaken and uncertain. This was home country, but he had never expected to feel so lost in it.

Once, as he was trying to decide what to do, he thought he heard Clarence calling. The sound was so very faint against the water's roar that he wasn't sure, but it brought a terrible longing just to see Clarence again and feel his comforting presence. He turned, almost ready to try the long climb back. But pain shot through his leg as he started to move, and he sank down again, shivering in the rain.

He had never been cold like this. Never in his life. Not even that time in his pup days when he had played tag under the ice with his family and some of the neighboring otter folk. What was wrong?

At last he realized that Clarence had spoken the truth about being civilized. He had been cooped up too long in that dratted steam-heated lab. Now he was so soft he couldn't even take a little spring rain. It was disgusting.

And to make it really rough, he probably had a broken leg.

With the thought that his injured leg might actually be broken, Swimmer's already sodden spirits began to sink still lower. How was he going to swim and catch food? How was he going to travel to different feeding grounds? And with dogs and wildcats to worry about, how could he protect himself?

As he considered these awful realities, he began to feel very sorry for himself. No matter how he looked at it, he was surely doomed. If he didn't die speedily of double pneumonia, he would have a lingering death from starvation, with his broken leg paining like fury to the last horrid minute.

"Oh, poor me," he whimpered. "Why did I ever leave Clarence?"

He was at rock bottom now and could sink no deeper. So, having enjoyed for a moment the very depths of despair, he wanted no more of it. It was time to climb out.

"Aw, fiffle," he muttered. "I've swallowed too much education, but I've still got a little frog sense. Anybody with half a grain of it ought to be able to beat the odds against him. Now, let's see . . ."

He still had one good swimming foot. It wouldn't push him fast enough to catch trout, but he could limp around and find crawfish and frogs. As for his bad leg, it had been injured on the lower part, so at least he could hold it off the ground when he walked and not have to drag it. If he was careful for a couple weeks, maybe it would mend.

What should he do in the meantime?

It struck him all at once that he had sort of upset Doc Hoffman's applecart by running away. Old Doc was going to be lost without his trained slave to show to the world, and furious to boot. In a matter of hours, sure as anything, there would be a big otter hunt on. Doc had money to burn. He would get men by the dozen. . . .

This chilling probability brought Swimmer to his feet. It was still raining, and the darkness had grayed only a trifle, but he knew he shouldn't waste any more time.

He began limping to the edge of the torrent. His intention was to follow the bank, find a quiet stretch where he could safely enter the water, then drift downstream. But he had taken only a few steps through the brush when a frightening thing happened.

The silver harness holding his bell caught on something sharp, and for long frantic seconds he was trapped. It was almost dawn when he finally freed himself and discovered that the sharp thing was a piece of rusted barbed wire. It was dangling from an overgrown fence.

Fuming, Swimmer tried desperately to squirm out of the dangerous harness. It was impossible. Had there been only the single chain about his neck that held the bell, he could have managed it easily. But there was a second chain behind his shoulders, and the two were linked tightly together. To get out of the dratted thing he would simply have to have help.

He crawled glumly under the fence and began limping downstream, the silver bell tinkling merrily with every painful movement. Since there was nothing he could do about the hateful sound, he tried to ignore it as he studied the creek. In the dawn mist the water didn't look quite so evil as the thunder of it in the dark had indicated. He crept down to the water, then hesitated while he tried to find the courage to enter it.

So much time had passed since he had been in a stream like this that for a moment Swimmer knew the old terror he had felt as a pup—the terror every pup feels before its mother forces it to swim. In the next breath fear was replaced by icy shock as he drove himself into the mist-laced current.

He gasped and grunted, sure that it would be the death of him. But after the first few minutes it didn't seem so bad. Then suddenly, for a little while, it was quite wonderful, and he found himself barking and chuckling happily, his injury nearly forgotten. Suddenly he glimpsed what he thought was a startled fish trying to dart away from him, and he made the mistake of trying to catch it. Such blinding pain shot through his leg that he was momentarily helpless.

He swam weakly to the farther bank and crawled out in a protected spot beneath an overhanging rock. Gradually the pain quieted. In its place came hunger.

His hunger increased through the morning, then grew teeth as he searched frantically along the bank, turning over small stones and driftwood in a hunt for something edible. Longingly he thought of the uneaten trout Clarence had brought him. It would have taken several trout that size to satisfy him now, but all he could find was one tiny frog that was hardly worth the painful effort of catching it.

"Aw, blatts!" he muttered finally, in weary disgust. "What am I going to do?"

He wasn't exactly frightened, but it was sort of jolting to realize that he was about as helpless as a month-old pup. What *was* he going to do?

Almost desperately he looked up at the wise old trees leaning overhead, something his mother always did when she wanted information. Had the trees seen others of the otter folk come this way? Did they know what he wanted to know? They did, and they told him—not with speech, but with a sort of flowing of knowledge they shared with all the wild who would listen.

Swimmer listened. It came to him that every stream too close to man has barren areas and that he was on the edge of them now. He must leave and cross the ridge to another creek. Others of his kind had been doing it for years. He might even find their trail.

Save for the rain, which had died to a misty drizzle, Swimmer might have missed the trail entirely. For the rain, instead of washing out a scent, holds it for a while and even makes it stronger.

Later that day, halfway across a sloping meadow where cows were grazing, he caught the first faint familiar scent of his own kind. It was so very faint in the deep grass that he was unable, in his present ignorance, to guess how long ago it had been made. But it hardly mattered. The otter folk were few in number, and it filled him with a great joy to know that some of them—several members of the same family, it seemed—were somewhere near.

He sprang forward, his miseries momentarily forgotten in his eagerness to get over the ridge and find the new creek. Then he realized he had been foolish to cross the meadow in daylight. All the cows were staring at him, attracted by the tinkling of his bell. The two nearer ones were actually coming to investigate.

It was too late to hide, so he put all his effort into reaching the woods ahead. Even when he was safe, with dense thickets behind him, he limped on. The lessons of the dim past were coming back to him. Where there were cows, he remembered, a dog was usually near.

Several times he was tempted to stop and search for

crawfish where small springs oozed from the ground. Caution drove him on. The otters ahead of him hadn't stopped. Perhaps they hadn't needed food, but more likely there were dangers near they didn't care to risk so far from water.

Darkness caught Swimmer near the top of the ridge. Almost mechanically he kept on for a while. When he finally stopped, it was because he had lost the trail and was too weary to search for it.

In his misery it seemed he had been climbing forever. Had it been this way in the past? Had his family changed streams and gone great distances and even crossed mountains to find new water?

But of course they had, as he now remembered. Only, it had been such fun in those days. They had always been playing and exploring, following an endless route around an area that must have been thirty miles across. In spite of the dangers it had been wonderful—until that blatted old snake-eyed trapper came with his net. . . .

Swimmer was having a horrid dream about that trapper when he was abruptly awakened by the yapping of a dog.

As his head jerked up he was shocked to discover that it was now bright daylight. How could he have slept so late? It was disgusting. No wild otter with the brains of a newt would have allowed himself to be caught out like this so far from water.

The dog yapped again, closer. Swimmer's impulse was to run, until he remembered his bell and realized the tinkling of it would give him away the moment he moved. From the yapping he decided that it was probably a small dog, one of those troublesome little busybodies of the kind that had belonged to the trapper.

He didn't know it was part of a hunting team until he saw the two does drifting past, as silently as shadows. At the sight of him the older doe paused briefly. Between them there was a quick exchange of thought.

The real danger, Swimmer learned, was not the dog but the human creature somewhere behind it.

It was time to leave. With the bell caught between his teeth, Swimmer began working his way cautiously downward in the direction of the new creek, whose rushing he could hear in the distance. Having to limp on three legs was bad enough, what with his empty belly and the way he was feeling, but being forced to do it with his head down, so he could hold the dratted bell, was almost too much.

Every few yards he stopped to test the air and listen. Even before he heard the human over on his left, he was suddenly startled by the feeling of deadly threat in that direction. He had forgotten that danger could be felt before it was seen or heard. Then he glimpsed it moving stealthily between the trees. The human was what Clarence would have called a tough-looking young punk in Levi's; he carried a gun and he was out to kill anything that moved.

"Drat 'em all!" Swimmer muttered angrily to himself. It was a crying shame the whole human race couldn't be done away with. Things would sure be better. Oh, he would want to save Clarence, of course, and probably Miss Primm. She had worked so hard teaching him. . . .

All at once the high yapping of the dog informed him that it must have stumbled across his scent. It was racing down toward him.

Swimmer dropped the bell and began leaping clumsily for the creek. He was only a few yards from it when the dog caught up with him and began yelping and circling in a frenzy. It was a nasty little brown mongrel no larger than himself; something about it was so infuriating to Swimmer that his blood boiled and he started to lunge for the dog.

But at that moment there was a hurried crashing in the underbrush and a yell from the dog's owner.

"Hang on to 'im, Tattle! Don't let 'im git away!"

Swimmer dodged in the direction of the creek, trying to keep trees and boulders between the gun and himself.

Somewhere in the distance a new voice—it sounded like a small girl's—cried shrilly, "Stop it, Weaver! Don't you dare shoot! You've no right—"

"I'll hunt where I danged please!" Weaver snapped. "You keep out of my business, or I'll bust you one!"

"Weaver—"

The girl's voice was lost in the roar of the gun. Chips of rock flew over Swimmer's head. The brown dog circled him swiftly, trying to turn him from the creek. It came an inch too close, and Swimmer made a single lightning snap that drove the dog away, yelping with pain.

As he scrambled down through the creek-side tangle, he was aware of Weaver's sudden furious burst of language, followed by a choking cry from the girl. It sounded as though she had been struck. Then the water closed over Swimmer's head and he was carried away by the current.

Downstream where the creek broadened and deepened, Swimmer surfaced briefly, his sleek dark head coming up and turning like a periscope. He was too shaken to see all that he might have seen, for his badly swollen leg was throbbing steadily and he was weak from hunger. All he wanted was a safe hiding place and a chance to find food. At the moment the only spot that seemed to offer shelter was a narrow crevice under an overhanging rock. He dove and swam to it.

It was a better place than he had expected. Only another otter could have found it. Way back under, a crack in the rock actually formed a dry shelf he could stretch out upon.

With the first small feeling of security he had felt since

leaving Clarence, Swimmer made himself as comfortable as he could on the shelf. Hunger gnawed at him, but that could wait till he had rested and calmed down a bit. There were trout in the pool, he could see them from the shelf. With a bit of scheming maybe he could catch one in spite of his bum leg. . . .

Abruptly all the woes of the world seemed to fall upon him. He felt homeless and lost and beaten and drowning in blackness. It was such an unspeakably awful feeling, as bad as that time when the trapper killed his mother, that it drove him out of his hiding place and back into the creek. Something was terribly wrong somewhere.

He surfaced cautiously in an eddy, and again his head came up like a periscope as he searched for danger. There was none. But over by the water's edge, huddled against a rock with her head in her arms, was a small redheaded girl. She was crying.

Swimmer had never seen a human cry before. Nor had he ever felt such desolation come from one. He was a little stunned.

Something in him melted. Slowly he swam to her.

At the water's edge he hesitated, trying to think of something soothing to say. But what can you say to a small human who can feel such black and utterly hopeless despair? He thought of inventing a few words, but none that came to mind seemed right for the occasion. Finally he crawled out beside her and nuzzled her arm, all the while making soft little chirruping sounds to show that he understood and sympathized.

The arm went about him instantly and clung tight. "Oh, Ripple," she sobbed, "I'm so glad you came. W-why does life have to be so—so awful?"

"Aw, it's not life. It's the dratted people in it," Swimmer mumbled, trying not to make his gnome voice sound so weary and gnomish. He hadn't intended to speak right away, fearing it would frighten her. The words just slipped out.

She wasn't frightened. But her sobbing stopped, and she turned her very freckled and tear-streaked face and stared at him. She had the brightest and unhappiest blue eye he had ever seen. He supposed the other eye was equally blue, but it was swollen shut and that side of her face was darkening.

"Why—why, you're not Ripple!" she said in wonder. "She hasn't learned to talk yet. Thank goodness you have. I —I need somebody to talk to so bad . . ."

"Is it because of the way that dirty Weaver treated you?"

"That's only part of it. How—how'd you know about Weaver?"

"Because I heard you yell at him when he and that ratty dog were after me."

"Oh!" she exclaimed. "It was *you* he shot at! He and his pa hate otters, and I was scared to death it was Ripple or her mother he was trying to kill." Suddenly her fingers discovered his harness. "Why, you're wearing a silver chain, and—and a bell! How beautiful! Do—do you belong to somebody?"

"Belong to somebody? Me?" Swimmer was outraged. "Phooey! I've been a prisoner in old Doc Hoffman's lab most of my life, and I just escaped the other night. And don't call this blatted bell beautiful. I hate it. It's a wonder that dirty Weaver didn't hear it, but with all the racket . . . Anyway, if I don't get rid of it soon, it'll surely be the death of me."

She stared at him again, and her good eye grew round and thoughtful. "Is—is your name Swimmer?"

"That's right. How'd you guess?"

"It was on TV last night," she said quickly. "I didn't hear

26

it all. You see, Mr. Sykes—I'm boarded out to Weaver's pa by the county 'cause I don't have folks—Mr. Sykes, he was mad at me as usual, and wouldn't let me listen. But—but there was something about a famous educated otter named Swimmer that was lost over in some other valley—"

She paused abruptly and gave a startled cry. "Oh! Your leg—you're hurt!"

In the next breath Swimmer was surprised to find her fussing over him like a vet. "I've fixed lots of breaks like this," she said. "Well, three, anyway. They were birds, but I can use the same sort of splint for you. A small piece of fresh poplar bark is best. It'll curl right around your leg, and I'll tie it real carefully. If you'll wait, I'll go get a knife and some string—"

They were interrupted by a man's voice calling angrily in the distance. "Penny? Where are you, Penny? Daggone you, girl, you'd better git back here fast!"

A sob caught in her throat, and she jumped to her feet. "That's Mr. Sykes," she whispered. "I—I have to run, but I'll try not to be long."

3

He Meets the Wild

For several minutes after Penny had gone, Swimmer waited uneasily on the rock, studying the wooded slope where he had seen her last. This part of the mountains was very different from the farming country he had come through yesterday. Everything was thicker and wilder, and there was hardly a sign that humans lived anywhere near. What, then, were people like Weaver Sykes and his father doing in this kind of place?

He was startled by the sudden excited cry of a kingfisher in the air directly behind him. It was a sound he had nearly forgotten. He turned in time to see the bird dive into the pool and emerge with a small fish in its bill.

The sight of food, caught so easily, was almost too much for the starving otter who had had only one undernourished frog to eat in two whole days. "Dratted cackle-head!" he muttered. "Do you have to show off in front of me?"

But maybe, if he went about it right, he could manage to snag a trout before Penny returned.

He slid back into the water. Cautiously he moved about the pool, keeping to the shadows. Several times he was able to creep close to trout, but they always darted to safety whenever he lunged for them. He was almost in despair when he discovered a crawfish hiding among the pebbles.

It was the most delicious bite he had ever had in his life. But it would have taken fifty such bites to ease the hunger that now raged in him, and he could find only two more crawfish in the pool. Instead of dulling his appetite, they whetted it. When he crawled back on the rock to wait for Penny, he felt hungrier than he had all day.

The afternoon shadows deepened. What could have happened to Penny? Worried now, he tested the air for sound and scent, searching for a clue that would tell more about her. But the breeze was wrong and all he caught was the whiff of a dog coming from the opposite direction.

It wasn't Tattle, the nuisance who had chased him. The scent was different. Something told Swimmer that the animal approaching was a much larger and more formidable creature. To be on the safe side, he crouched on the edge of the rock, ready to slide into the pool.

The dog appeared suddenly, without a sound—a big tawny beast with powerful jaws and heavy shoulders, eyes as hard and sharp as polished flint. It studied Swimmer a moment, then gave a low growl that was more of a greeting than a threat.

You are new here? The thought was as clear as speech.

Yes, Swimmer responded. *You know others of my kind?*

I know all who come through here. Her friends are my friends.

There wasn't any doubt that Penny was meant. *It is a relief to know you are on her side,* Swimmer admitted. *She really needs a friend like you. If you had only been here earlier . . .*

I was far away when I felt the trouble in her. What happened?

Swimmer explained. The dog growled again, this time in

29

anger, and turned to go up the slope where Penny had gone. But he had taken only a few steps when it became evident that someone was coming.

Instantly the big dog gave a happy bark and sprang into the shadows. In a few seconds Swimmer heard Penny exclaim, "Scruff, you old dickens, you! Oh, I'm so glad to see you! Where've you been?"

When they came out by the creek, Penny said, "Swimmer, I came back as soon as I could, but I had to help Mr. Sykes pack another rush order. Then I had an awful time of it sneaking away with all the things I needed without being caught. The way they watch me, you'd think I was a thief."

She started to open a paper bag she carried, then suddenly exclaimed, "My goodness, I haven't introduced you two! Scruff, this is Swimmer. He's been in captivity a long time, but he's just escaped and he's got a broken leg. You've got to promise to be his friend, Scruff. Swimmer—"

"We've already met," Swimmer interrupted. "And he's told me that your friends are his friends."

Penny stared at him. "Scruff *talked* to you?"

"Well, sort of. We exchanged thoughts."

"Honestly?" Her small mouth grew round.

"Sure," said Swimmer. "Everything exchanges thoughts. Except people, of course. They're sort of limited."

She giggled. Then, seriously, "I know Scruff's awfully smart. He understands every word I say, even though he's a wild dog and won't go near anyone but me. But being smart doesn't make him a mind reader. If he was, he'd know exactly what I've got in this bag."

"But of course he knows! So do I!"

"Tell me!"

"String, knife, pliers, and—and four trout."

Penny blinked her good eye and suddenly laughed. "Aw,

but I'd already told you part of what I was going to bring. And you smelled the trout."

"Pshaw, I can't smell in numbers. And you didn't say anything about bringing pliers." The tantalizing smell of the fish was becoming almost more than Swimmer could bear. "Please," he begged. "Won't you give me a trout before I have a fainting spell? I can't catch 'em with a bum leg and I'm starved to a frazzle."

"Oh, you poor thing!" Instantly she drew a fat trout from the bag and placed it on the rock before him. A second trout went to Scruff. "I had a feeling you'd be back," she said to the dog, "so I stole an extra fish for you. I'm saving the two little ones for Willow and Ripple—not that they're hungry, but they do love to be remembered."

"You stole them?" Swimmer burbled between bites.

"I sure did. Mr. Sykes runs a trout farm." Her mouth tightened defiantly. "Maybe I *am* a thief, but I don't care. I work hard enough to pay for ten times a few fish. The minute I'm back from school it's, Penny, do this; Penny, do that; Penny, do something else. Wash the dishes, make the beds, iron the shirts, fix the supper—and, in between, it's always the trout. I've just finished cleaning and packing a hundred and fifty trout for that rush order that came in this afternoon."

While she spoke, she had been examining a clump of poplar saplings that grew near the bottom of the slope. Now she drew a knife from the bag and made two cuts around a smooth section of one of the slender trunks. Carefully she peeled away the bark between the cuts, then knelt beside Swimmer and began trimming the bark to fit the broken leg.

Her small, quick hands were as gentle as could be, and in less than a minute she had the leg firmly and comfortably encased in a tube of bark. Not once did she really hurt him, even while straightening the leg in the splint or tying it securely afterward. But Swimmer could not resist an occasional agonized groan just to get her sympathy.

"You're a living doll," he murmured, conscious of Scruff's jealousy as she fussed over him and more than ever aware of what a skinny little mistreated thing she was. Miss Primm back at the lab would have been shocked at the sight of her bruised face, and thoroughly scandalized by the ragtag dress and the woebegone scrap of ribbon that held back her red hair. Swimmer's heart went out to her.

After catching the thought from Scruff, he said, "Scruff wants you to know that if he ever finds Weaver out in the woods, he'll chew him apart."

"No!" Penny cried instantly. "Don't you dare! Scruff, that would be the end of everything. If Weaver didn't shoot at you, somebody else would. You know how they feel about wild dogs around here." She paused and began shaking her finger at both of them for emphasis. "Don't either of you ever, ever, go near the place up there. If you're seen, they'll shoot you on sight. And, Swimmer, they hate otters like poison. So stay away from the trout ponds, and don't even go wading in that little branch that drains them."

"What's wrong with it?"

"It's full of traps."

"Traps!"

"Yes. Those horrible steel things with jaws. Most of the branch is on this side of the fence, on government land, but that doesn't make any difference. Not to an old meanie like Grady Sykes. You'd think he owned everything in the forest preserve. Anyway, I always spring every trap I can find, and I'd throw it away if I could. Only, he makes sure every trap is chained to something. Usually to a metal stake, and they're terribly hard to pull out of the ground."

She paused and added in a low voice, "Mr. Sykes caught

me trying to pull one loose last fall, and gave me an awful licking. I—I almost ran away."

"Why didn't you?"

"I didn't have any place to go. And besides, I hated to leave my friends. Scruff and Ripple and Willow are the best in the world. They're on the move a lot, but they spend most of their time here. A person *has* to have friends. So I decided I'd just tough it out a while and maybe something good would happen." All at once she smiled happily and clapped her hands. "And it did! You came along. Now, I've got a friend who can really talk to me and help me understand the others. I think it's wonderful."

Swimmer did too. He grasped her hand and practically purred.

Penny said, "I'll call the others in a minute, but first let's see what I can do about your bell and harness."

She took the pliers from the sack and began working at one of the heavy links on his shoulder. Her mouth tightened as she began to pull and twist.

"I—I can't do a thing with one pair of pliers," she admitted finally. "I'll have to get a second pair to hold the chain, or else use a hacksaw. But maybe, if I help, you can sort of wiggle out of it."

They tried. Swimmer squirmed and twisted and did his utmost to get one leg through the harness. It was impossible.

"Don't worry," Penny assured him. "I'll get it off tomorrow, somehow. Tomorrow's Sunday, so there's no telling when I can slip away, but I'll come just as soon as I can. Now, let's see if I can find Ripple and Willow."

She crept down to the water's edge, found a small round stone, and began tapping it sharply on the side of a half submerged boulder. She would tap three times, wait a few seconds, and tap three times again. In spite of the rushing water the sound could be heard for a long distance.

Presently, when there was no response to her signal, she climbed back beside him. "They must be downstream," she said. "Let's go down past the bend to the old beech tree. I think they've got a secret den under the tree where they sleep, but I'm not sure. Anyway, they're bound to be near there." Then she glanced at his bark-encircled leg and exclaimed, "Oh, my goodness! Maybe you don't feel like going anywhere."

To tell the truth, Swimmer didn't. It was the hour when broken bones always begin to ache and weary bodies long for rest. But these matters became as nothing beside the electrifying thought of actually meeting some of his own kind again. Swimmer trembled with sudden anticipation.

"Let's go," he said eagerly.

It would have been much easier for him to swim the distance, but he wouldn't have had the fun of being with her and talking. So he went limping painfully along at her side while Scruff trotted ahead, a guard ever on the alert for danger.

It took only a few minutes to reach the mouth of the branch that drained the pools at the trout farm. After they had crossed it on stepping-stones, Swimmer paused and studied it almost longingly, for it reminded him of the pleasant waters he had played in as a pup. The branch came down through the rocky tangle in a series of enticing little falls that begged to be explored.

"Wow!" Swimmer exclaimed. "What a place for crawfish!"

"And *traps*," Penny reminded him tartly. "Weaver's pa, he's as sly as anything about setting a trap. You can't see it, and he hides it right where you'd put your foot. You'll never get Willow in there again."

"Why not?"

"I—I'd rather not talk about it." She swallowed and turned away. "We'd better hurry. It's getting late."

But the tragic picture that had come to Penny's mind was entirely too vivid for Swimmer to miss. It was a bitter winter scene with an otter frozen in the ice of a small pool, one foot caught in a trap. Another otter crouched near it, crying.

Swimmer could not help asking, "Was it Willow's mate you found?"

She gasped and stared at him, then nodded slowly.

"It was last winter," she told him. "If it hadn't snowed and turned so mean and cold afterward, maybe I could have found him in time to save him. But it dropped 'way below zero, and I couldn't come down here and see how everybody was 'cause I didn't have boots and a coat. But, please, let's don't talk about it."

For a while they moved along in silence. Then Swimmer asked curiously, "Has Ripple got a brother?"

"Why, yes! How did you guess?"

"On the way here yesterday I was following an old trail made by others of my kind. Two of them must have been Willow and Ripple. But I was sure there was a third."

"Oh, that was Splasher. He's a perfect rascal! You'd never guess what he did. When he came back last week he didn't pay a bit of attention to my warning. Instead, he slipped up to the house, gave his little bark to let me know who he was, then dashed to the trout ponds and tore through them like crazy. Why, he scared those poor fish out of their ever-loving minds—they were jumping all over the place! Of course, he did it just to devil Mr. Sykes. And I never saw Mr. Sykes so hopping mad. He yelled for Tattle and grabbed his shotgun and started blasting away at where the trout were jumping—and all he did was to kill a bucketful of his own fish. And Splasher got clean away."

She giggled and added, "It was awfully foolish of him to take such a chance, and, of course, I bawled him out afterward. But I know how he felt. The funny thing is that Mr. Sykes thinks the otters are stealing him blind, but they're not. Golly, Splasher wouldn't even touch a trout if he could find enough crawfish. Would you?"

"I'm all for crawfish," Swimmer affirmed. "But it's precious few I've had in recent years. Where's Splasher now?"

"Down the creek somewhere. I haven't seen him since Monday, so I think he's gone to hunt for a mate." She stopped. "Here's the beech."

Swimmer peered up with awe and deep respect at the great trunk spreading its branches over a wide stretch of the creek. It wasn't the biggest tree he had ever seen, but it was certainly the oldest. He could feel its age as its sheltering leaves whispered a welcome to him, telling of the countless feathered ones who had nested under that arching roof, and of the generations of his own kind who had taken refuge in its secret hollows. One glance at the beckoning tangle of roots dipping down into the water and he could almost see the hiding places under the huge trunk.

Penny scrambled down to the water's edge and began tapping on a rock. At the first signal two sleek dark heads periscoped at the far end of the pool then streaked toward her, barking and chirruping happily. As they reached the bank she leaned forward, laughing, and touched noses with each of them.

"Willow, Ripple," she began. "I've brought a new friend to meet you. His name is Swimmer. He's been a prisoner a long time, but he's just escaped and he's got a broken leg. Please be nice to him, 'cause he really needs help."

Willow and her daughter came up the bank, eyes bright

and curious while they briefly touched noses with him. Swimmer, momentarily forgetting his aches, burbled with happiness. It was pure heaven to be with his own kind again, even though one was a plump matron years older than himself, and the other a skinny teen-ager.

Little questioning thoughts flowed swiftly between them. Slender Ripple, more impulsive than her mother, became fascinated by Swimmer's bell, and gave a delighted laugh, which was almost like Penny's, when it rang to her touch.

"You wouldn't like it if you had to wear one of the dratted things," he told Ripple aloud.

Willow and Ripple looked at him in astonishment.

You speak as she speaks! came the awed thought from Ripple. *How did you learn?*

From being so long around humans.

Do you think I could learn? Ripple asked.

Why would you want to?

So I could talk to her. We understand her, but she does not understand us. It would be so much more fun if she could.

Penny took the two small trout from the bag, and Willow and Ripple accepted them with little sounds of pleasure that were more affected than real, as he quickly learned. They preferred wild trout to tame ones, which had no flavor. *But don't tell her,* they warned. *We wouldn't think of hurting her feelings.*

Swimmer hadn't had a real wild trout for so long that he had almost forgotten the difference. He watched them stand up and neatly clip the tails and fins before beginning to eat. But they had hardly taken the first delicate bites when Scruff, who had been resting quietly under the tree, suddenly sprang to his feet with a low growl.

"Someone's coming!" Penny whispered. "Quick, everybody hide!"

4

He Learns His Value

At the first hint of danger, even before Penny spoke, Willow and Ripple had turned and slipped quietly into the water, hardly disturbing its surface. Swimmer followed clumsily and was barely in time to glimpse them vanishing in the blackness under the great tree's roots. Seconds later he emerged in a dim and curiously curved chamber with a thin ray of light coming from somewhere above. The beech tree was partially hollow. The hollow area seemed to extend upward to a hole high in the trunk.

Swimmer crawled out and crouched in a dry corner opposite Willow and Ripple. In his sudden uneasiness he tried to read the thoughts of those outside, but all he learned was that Scruff had caught the scent of an approaching human, a stranger.

Don't be afraid, Willow offered comfortingly. *It is probably only a fisherman.*

It's not a fisherman, he told her. *The person coming has something to do with me. I feel it.*

He glanced up at the hole where the light came through, and realized all at once that he ought to be able to reach it with very little trouble. The tree leaned sharply in the direction of the hole, and there were plenty of places to cling to along the way.

It took only a few painful seconds to make the climb, and when he peered through the opening he discovered that he was not in the main part of the tree at all, but in a huge limb that curved away from it. Penny and Scruff were almost directly below.

Suddenly Scruff took a few steps forward and growled again. Penny caught him around the neck and clung to him. "Please, Scruff!" she ordered. "You've got to be good." Then to someone in the distance, "It's all right, mister. I won't let him hurt you."

"Lordy me, I hope not," replied the unseen one. "Tell you what. If he won't bite me, I'll cross my heart and solemnly promise not to bite him. Is it a deal?"

"It's a deal," Penny giggled.

At the first sound of that familiar voice, Swimmer almost slipped from his perch. It just couldn't be—but it was. He pressed his face closer to the hole and presently saw a barely recognizable Clarence come into view. The dapper city-Clarence had turned into an outdoorsman in paratrooper's boots and khakis, with a sleeping bag over one shoulder and a knapsack over the other. The black man seemed tired, for he leaned heavily on a hiking staff cut from a sapling.

"I'm Clarence Green," he began. "What's your name, young lady?"

"Penny," she told him. "Penny Jones. I mean, that's what Welfare calls me. I haven't a real name."

"It's real enough for me. I like it. That sure is some dog you've got there. But he ought to have a collar on him."

"Scruff's wild. He wouldn't stand for a collar."

"You mean really wild?" Clarence backed away.

"He sure is. I'm his only friend. But don't be afraid, 'cause he won't bother my friends."

Clarence chuckled. "Believe me, I'll be careful to stay on the right side of you! Er, have you many wild friends?"

"Lots of 'em. Well, four or five, anyway."

"H'mm. Would any of them be otters?"

Penny gaped at him. "How—how'd you guess?"

"Oh, I'm good at guessing. Looks like I've finally reached the right place."

"Right—right place for what?" Penny asked uncertainly.

"It's a long story," Clarence said. "Just let me sit down and rest my tired bones a while and I'll tell you."

Up in the tree, Swimmer was having some difficulty with his emotions. One moment he wanted to rush down happily and greet Clarence, and the very next he wished he could be a thousand miles away. But he couldn't think of going anywhere until his leg mended. And besides, there was Penny.

Could she keep a secret? She'd try, of course—but Clarence was one smart cookie.

Ripple asked, *Do you know the stranger?*

Yes, he admitted. *He cared for me when I was a prisoner.*

Below him Clarence removed the gear from his shoulders and sank down with a sigh. He offered Penny a chocolate bar, which she accepted gratefully. Then he unfolded a map and studied it a few seconds.

"Do you live near here, young lady?"

"I'm not a lady yet. Just call me Penny."

"Okay—if you'll call me Clarence. Is it a deal?"

She giggled and sat down. "It's a deal."

"Then here's another chocolate bar to bind it. There's lots more, because it's all I take to eat on a hike. Now, let's see. I'll bet you live at Sykes's trout farm. Is that right?"

"You guessed right again." She smiled and pointed. "It's

up yonder a little way." She added quickly, "I—I'll have to be going soon, 'cause it's getting late and I'll have to help with supper."

"Well, I sure don't want you to be late, for I've heard they're sort of ornery. Was it one of them that hit you?"

She nodded. "I'm sure glad Scruff didn't see it, or something terrible would have happened. What—what were you going to tell me?"

"Did you ever hear of an otter named Swimmer?"

"Swimmer!" she exclaimed, and Scruff's ears perked up and he gave a little bark.

"So you've already found him," Clarence said slowly. "I knew I'd come to the right place."

Penny sprang to her feet and cried, "I know all about Swimmer, 'cause I heard it in the news. But I didn't say I'd found him. You—you've just been pumping me, an' I'm not going to talk to you any more!"

She turned quickly and started away, her small chin high.

"Wait!" Clarence called. "Please—I'm Swimmer's friend. He's in trouble, and I've come to help him."

Penny stopped. "How do I know you're his friend?"

"You could ask him. I'm the man who used to take care of him. I was driving the van when he ran away."

"You—you just want to catch him an' put him in a cage again!"

"No!" Clarence protested. "But I simply must see him and talk to him. It's important."

She came back and crouched near the tree again.

"Honest?" she pleaded. "Are you telling me the truth?"

"Honest, cross my heart," answered Clarence most solemnly and crossed his heart as he spoke.

"Aw'right. But how—how'd you happen to come straight here?"

"Penny, I didn't come straight here. I've been following

41

my nose ever since Swimmer ran away. First thing I did was go to the Forest Service office and get a map. Soon as I saw Otter Creek here, and saw that it ran through forest preserve all the way to the river, something buzzed in my head. Ever get that funny feeling in your head when you know something's true, even though you can't prove it?"

"Sure, lots of times. Well, two or three, anyway."

"Well, that's how it was with me. Something buzzed in my head. There had to be a reason, I said, why a creek was named Otter instead of Eagle or Bear or ninety other names. You see?"

"Of course!" Penny exclaimed. "It's because otters have always come to it. And they come to it because there's something about it they like. Big pools, crawfish . . ."

"Right. And after taking a good look at that first stream where he escaped, I figured it wouldn't be long before Swimmer left it for better water. So this morning early I drove to Otter Creek Bridge downstream, left the van there, and started hiking upstream."

"Why, that's miles and *miles!*"

"And no distance at all by road," Clarence muttered. "If I'd just started up here first . . . But no matter. I didn't find fresh otter signs till I reached the beaver pond around the bend yonder. But the freshest signs of all are right here on that rock. See?"

Clarence pointed to the neatly clipped tails and fins near the water. "You were watching somebody you know eat a trout not twenty minutes ago. Was it Swimmer?"

"It—it was Willow and Ripple. I brought them some fish."

"But Swimmer was here too, wasn't he?"

"I—I—please, don't ask me."

"But I've got to see him, Penny."

"I can't help it. I—I shouldn't say another word about

42

him until—until I have his permission. It wouldn't be fair."

"That means you've already seen him and talked to him. Right?"

"Y—yes," Penny said faintly.

Up in the tree, Swimmer clung grumpily to his perch, a little upset by Clarence's questioning. Old slick tongue! he thought. He'll get every blatted thing out of her.

Suddenly Penny said, "If you don't intend to take him back with you, *why* have you got to see him?"

"Because I'm worried about him," Clarence admitted. "I'm worried sick. He doesn't belong here, Penny. He's become civilized. He's not used to being out like this. It would be so easy for him to catch pneumonia and die. And I keep feeling he's hurt. It was stormy when he left the van, and I thought the door slammed on him. If he's hurt, I ought to get him to a vet . . ."

Clarence stopped, then asked, "Is he hurt, Penny?"

"A—a little," she faltered.

"What's wrong?"

"He—he—he's got a broken leg," she burst out. And at the shocked look on Clarence's face, she added in a rush, "But I fixed it! I'm real good at that. Well, pretty good, anyway. I put a bark splint all around it, and that's a lot better'n what a vet would do. There wasn't anything else wrong with him 'cept that he was awfully hungry, 'cause it's so hard for him to catch food. So I gave him the biggest fish I could find, then introduced him to Willow and Ripple. They'll take care of him and show him the best places to hide."

She paused for breath, adding quickly, "So you see, he's going to be perfectly all right. You needn't worry about him at all."

"But he's *not* going to be all right!" Clarence exclaimed,

getting unsteadily to his feet. "By this time tomorrow there'll be men out looking all over the place for Swimmer. Doc Hoffman's promised a big reward to anyone who finds him. On top of that he's hiring the best hunter and trapper in the mountains. That fellow will trail him straight here with a bloodhound."

"But—but that doesn't mean he'll be caught."

"Why, sakes alive, with a broken leg Swimmer won't have a chance. He might even be killed. That trapper's a brute!"

"But how can anyone find him in the creek if he stays hidden? Won't they think he's gone on downstream?"

"Lordy, I hope so." Clarence snapped his fingers worriedly. "I don't know what to do. Seems like there ought to be a safer place for him than here. Honestly, the best thing would be for me to take him back to Doc Hoffman's lab. Then he wouldn't get hurt again, and I—"

"No!"

"Now, don't get me wrong," Clarence hastened to say. "I wouldn't take him anywhere against his will—not after the way he saved my neck the other night." There followed an account of the van's near-accident. Clarence continued, "I've been looking after Swimmer ever since I retired from the army. He's about the only family I've got. It sure upsets a person . . ." He looked at her curiously. "How'd you manage to find him?"

"I didn't find him. He found me."

"Say that again?"

"That's how it was. It happened after Weaver Sykes hit me, and I was wishing I was dead, 'cause I didn't have anywhere to go or anyone to talk to—and that's when Swimmer came up and started to sympathize. He knew exactly how I felt."

"It didn't throw you when he started to talk?"

44

"Goodness, no. I always thought Ripple could talk if only I had time to teach her. Anyway, it was wonderful to find a friend. Otters are ever so much nicer than people. I—I just wish I were one."

"Penny," Clarence said slowly. "You're a mighty special person, and you share a big secret with me."

"What's that?"

"We're the only ones in the world who know that Swimmer can talk."

"Really?"

"Yeah. And we're going to keep it a secret. If Doc Hoffman knew it, he'd throw a fit. And Miss Primm—that's his teacher—why, she'd fall through the floor. As for everybody else . . ."

Clarence shook his head. "Penny, I don't know what to do, but if we work together, maybe we can figure out something. Er, how far is it to the bridge by road?"

" 'Bout two miles."

"That's too far to hike this evening, the way I feel. Guess I'd better camp here tonight and bring the van around in the morning. You know that old timber road on the left, just before you reach the trout farm?"

"Sure. But you can't go far on it."

"It doesn't matter. I just want to park the van out of sight. Say, when I was cruising around yesterday, trying to get the country straight in my mind, I had a quick look at the trout farm. Mighty pretty little place—but how come that Sykes bunch is running it?"

"They just inherited it," Penny said. "But I'm afraid the bank's going to get it soon."

"How's that?"

"I think they borrowed too much money to buy cars and things, and now they can't pay it back. I—I'll sure hate to leave, 'cause I'll never see my friends again."

"Oh, maybe you will."

"I don't see how—unless I run away and take my friends with me."

"That's an interesting idea," Clarence said slowly. "Let's think about it. It's about sundown, so you'd better get on back to the house. I don't want to see you with another black eye tomorrow."

For a minute after Penny and Scruff had gone, Swimmer remained by the hole, digesting what he had heard. It gave him an entirely new view of things. Finally, after Clarence had moved out of sight, he crept painfully back to the floor of the hollow.

Willow and Ripple looked at him curiously. Thoughts flashed between them.

Is it safe outside now?

It is safe. The black man is still there, but he is my friend.

Then we will go and play in the pools until dark. We wish you could come with us. It's always more fun when three can play together.

Swimmer told them it would be many days before he could play. *But I'll follow you out,* he added. *I must talk to my friend.*

He was so tired and full of hurts that he hated even to move again. But after a few minutes to build up his gumption, he forced himself into the water and surfaced by one of the rocks under the tree.

Clarence was somewhere downstream. Faintly above the sound of the creek, Swimmer could hear him calling, "Swimmer? Where are you, Swimmer? Please come out!"

Swimmer's first inclination was to paddle down to Clarence with the current. But on second thought he climbed out over the rocks and began limping slowly along the game trail that followed the stream.

46

Before many more hours, sure as day and night, some gloopy hound would pick up his scent at the other creek and follow it here. It would be downright stupid to allow the scent to stop at the beech tree. To leave a good false trail, of course, he would have to swim back to the tree. But that was a detail he could worry about later.

Suddenly he caught sight of Clarence in an open spot ahead. He tried to call out, but at that instant something seemed to go wrong with his throat. He couldn't even manage a froggy squawk. But Clarence turned, evidently attracted by the tinkling of the bell. There was a gasped "Glory be!" and he came on the run.

It was really great to have old Clarence make such a fuss over him. The splinted leg came in for a world of attention. "Yessir," said Clarence, nodding, "that Penny, she did a mighty fine job on you! She's a wonderful kid. I had a long talk with her. If you'd just come a little earlier—"

"Oh, I heard you," Swimmer admitted. "I—I heard all you said."

"You *what?*"

"I was up in a hollow tree, and I eaves—eaves—what's the blatted word?"

"Eavesdropped."

"That's right. I eavesdropped. I couldn't help it. I—"

"You didn't have to hide, for Pete's sake! Why didn't you come out?"

"Because I knew what you were thinking. You were thinking, dong ding it, that the best place for me was back at the lab, and I was afraid—"

"It *is* the best place for you," Clarence insisted. "But I'll never take you there unless you're willing to go."

"What about your job?"

Clarence chuckled. "Doc hit the ceiling when I phoned him you'd escaped. He told me never to come back unless I brought you with me. Pshaw, I don't need a job. I'm a retired army sergeant with a pension. Anyway, you've upset the applecart, and Doc's having a howling tizzy. He's offering a big reward for you."

"How much?"

"Twenty thousand dollars."

Swimmer had little regard for money and he was not impressed. "Aw, fiffle!" he muttered, like a disgusted gnome. "He paid seven times that for a galumping horse that can't do anything but look pretty in a picture."

"It's a palomino," said Clarence, "and Doc thinks he looks pretty riding it. But you miss the point, old pal. To a poor guy who's never seen much money, twenty thousand dollars is a whale of a wad. Up in this country it'll look like a million. By tomorrow these mountains will be crawling with folks carrying everything from nets to pitchforks. Lord help any poor otter they happen to see!"

"I'll be safe. I'm with friends. We've a great place to hide."

"Yeah?" Clarence cocked a shrewd eye at him. "It wouldn't be back yonder under that big old beech tree, would it?"

"Oops! How'd you guess?"

"Pshaw, I was raised in the country. The tree looked like a good place, and those trout fins near it were a dead giveaway." Clarence scowled. "We'll have to get rid of those fins. And maybe I'd better go back and make camp under the tree—at least until we've figured out the best thing to do. It'll sort of throw people off if they find me camping there."

"What about this dratted bell and harness? Can you get 'em off for me?"

"Not without tools. It'll have to wait till I bring the van over in the morning."

Swimmer glanced uneasily at the creek. Here the water

was racing down into another big pool, frothing white in places where it smashed against rocks. How could he ever fight his way back to the tree against all that rush of water? Yet he hadn't gone half as far as he should to leave a decent false trail.

He explained his problem to Clarence. "We're both sort of beat," he said. "But if I can make it as far as the beaver pond, will you carry me back to the beech tree?"

Clarence groaned, but nodded. "It's a deal, old pal."

5

He Sees an Old Enemy

With the coming of night it was pleasant to be back in the snug den, with Willow and Ripple near, and Clarence dozing in a sleeping bag just outside. He couldn't hear Clarence, but he was very much aware of his comforting presence; occasionally he could even catch the faint odor of woodsmoke from the small campfire as it drifted past the hole above. A cricket chirped near the hole, and back in the unexplored chambers under the tree he could hear the faint squeaks and rustlings of tiny rodents. All other sounds were lost in the steady crash and rush of the stream.

Gradually the aching in his leg subsided, and he slept. But it was a troubled sleep, filled with vague dreams that became more unpleasant as the dawn approached. He awoke suddenly, and found that all the contentment he had known earlier had fled. In its place was uneasiness.

Just below him the tunnel of water leading outside was turning from black to blue, and a thin shaft of greenish light was filtering down from the hole above. He knew without having to look that Clarence was gone. At the same instant he was aware that Willow and Ripple were watching him, and that they shared his uneasiness.

Is there danger? they asked.

Not yet, he replied. *It is far away, but I feel it coming.*

Now he could feel the uncertainty in Willow. The den was important to her. It had always been her main refuge, and her children had been born here. But if trouble were on the way, wouldn't it be better to leave?

Do you know of a better hiding place? he asked.

The creek has many places to hide, but this is the best. It has another entrance.

Swimmer hadn't even thought of such a possibility. The other entrance, he learned, was downstream in what may once have been a woodchuck burrow, though various other creatures had been known to use it.

Then we will stay here, he told them. *Soon strangers will come, searching. We must be very careful not to be seen, or even to leave a sign of ourselves around.*

He wondered how he was going to manage about food. But maybe after he got rid of the bell and harness, he would be able to move a little faster and snag an occasional hornyhead chub. They weren't as quick as trout. And there were the cases of canned fish that were always carried for him in the van. Clarence had promised to bring some tins of tuna, after the van was driven around from the bridge. That would be a big help, of course, except that he couldn't expect Clarence to be on hand every time he got hungry.

A bit enviously he watched Willow slip into the water and dart out into the brightening pool to catch her breakfast. Ripple started to follow, but paused before him and playfully tapped his bell. Again, at its tinkling, she gave the little sound of delight that was so much like Penny's laughter. Impulsively, she touched her nose to his and darted outside.

Swimmer was still tingling from that touch when Ripple returned, bringing two fish, one in her mouth and the other firmly grasped in her nimble "hands." She placed the larger fish before him and settled down beside him to eat the other.

Swimmer overflowed with an emotion he had never felt before, and his heart went out to her.

Penny did not appear that morning, nor did Clarence return. Swimmer's uneasiness grew. According to his figuring —and he had a flawless sense of time to go with his abhorred training in mathematics—Clarence should have been back before the sun was three hours high. That was making all sorts of allowances, like an extra fifteen minutes to climb to the county road that went past the trout farm, plus an extra half hour to hike to the bridge.

But when Clarence did not appear by noon, Swimmer twisted worriedly in his harness and came to an unhappy conclusion: The delay was caused by something unforeseen and decidedly unpleasant.

It was less than an hour later that a new feeling of danger sent him up to keep watch at his peephole. He was hardly settled when Willow and her daughter slipped back into the den with the news that several young humans and a dog were approaching.

Swimmer almost groaned when he heard a familiar yapping. Presently Tattle dashed past, hard upon a scent. Behind him, carrying his gun, came Weaver Sykes. With him were two gangling youths armed with some sticks, a gunnysack, and a piece of rope.

"Yeah, Pa claims all this land down here," Weaver Sykes was saying as they paused under the tree. "But I reckon he won't mind your hunting if it's an otter you're after—that is, as long as you don't hunt upstream from here. He wouldn't like that."

"But what about the reward?" the taller youth asked. "If

we catch the critter, reckon he'd want us to give 'im part of the money?"

"Reward? Who said anything about a reward? How much is it?"

"Well, we heard at church this morning it was twenty thousand dollars. But right off folks figgered that was a mistake, an' that somebody'd just put the decimal point in the wrong place. They said that more'n likely it was two thousand. But that's plenty."

"Two thousand dollars for a danged dirty fish-stealin' varmint?" Weaver exclaimed. "Why, anybody who'd pay that is clean out'n his cotton-pickin' mind!"

"But, Weaver, it's a famous otter. They say it even wears a silver harness an' a bell."

"I don't care what it wears. It's still a danged varmint an' it ain't worth *that* much."

"Shucks, nobody said it was. But you know them rich flatlanders. They'd pay anything for something they want."

"Reckon you're right," Weaver admitted. "But how come you're looking here for the varmint? They say it escaped 'way across the ridge on Red Dog Creek."

"Aw, there ain't no fish in Red Dog. An' the warden says a traveling otter always leaves the lower part of it an' heads this way." The youth turned and started down to the water's edge. "C'mon, Joe. There's a mess of holes around here. If I poke the critter out, you gotta be ready to bop 'im on the head. You gonna help us, Weaver?"

"No," Weaver muttered. "Daggone! Two thousand dollars! I better tell Pa about this." He moved away suddenly and began to run back the way he had come.

Tattle returned a moment later, but instead of following Weaver, the dog began leaping about the tree, yapping in a frenzy.

Oh, blatts! Swimmer thought despairingly. It was my

trail he was following all the time. Now, he's trying to find out if I'm here. That sneaky little hunk of buzzard bait!

Down at the creek's edge one of the hunters cried, "Shaddup, you fool dog! You tryin' to scare everything away?"

"Mebbe he's tryin' to tell us there's something in the tree," the other said.

They waded over and began thrusting their sticks down under the roots. Almost immediately they found the underwater entrance to the den, but the exploring sticks could reach no farther than a rock around which the passageway curved.

"If anything was here," grumbled one, "it got scared away earlier." He pointed to the remains of Clarence's fire. "Somebody camped there last night. We'd better go on down the creek."

The two hurried away. But Tattle remained, yapping, snarling, and finally breaking into an urgent high-pitched barking that could be heard for a great distance.

At the sound of it Swimmer chilled. As soon as Weaver or his father became aware of that telltale barking, they'd come on the run and there would be real trouble. At the thought of what could happen to Willow and Ripple, his lips drew back in a snarl and the hair began to rise on his neck. He crept down from his perch.

I must get rid of the nuisance, he told Ripple.

I will help you, she said instantly.

Thoughts flashed between them. His bell was the main problem. Because of it he couldn't make an attack until the last possible instant, when the dog was within easy reach. Nor must they touch the ground and leave a fresh scent for other dogs to find.

We will make a game of it, she said. *I will attract his attention. You do the rest.*

So it became a game. Ripple swam out first and flashed

54

into the current, moving and turning with a grace and speed that no fish could equal. Swimmer followed slowly and crept with the utmost stealth to the edge of a pebbly spot just beyond the largest rock. Here he flattened in the shadow, with only his face above the surface. At a glance he might have been only a part of the rock itself.

Now Ripple darted in close and spun about in the shallows chirruping gaily. Tattle saw her on the instant, and for a second his mouth hung open as if he could not believe his eyes. Then he dashed down to the pebbly spot, snarling.

A wiser dog than Tattle, even if he had been twice the size, would have hesitated at the water's edge and would not have taken another step. For in the water, as Swimmer well knew, an otter is supreme. Nothing could have touched Ripple, so she was entirely without fear as she paused in the shallows and laughed. This infuriated Tattle, and he made the mistake of his life—he sprang into the shallows after her.

Swimmer had been hoping for this. Instantly, with all the power he could force into his three good legs, he lunged for Tattle's throat.

Unfortunately his harness caught on a spur of rock, throwing him off-balance. He missed the throat entirely but was quick enough to sink his teeth into a leg. It was sufficient. Tattle had time only for a frightened shriek before he was jerked down into deep water.

Swimmer held on grimly and let the swift current carry them downstream. The dog struggled violently at first, then its motions became feeble.

Suddenly from Ripple, who was circling easily around them, came the thought: *Do not kill.*

In Swimmer's private opinion, Tattle was much too low and contemptible a creature to be allowed to live, and something told him he would regret it if he let the nuisance

55

go. But it was not his nature to kill for the sake of killing. He had subdued his enemy, and that was enough.

He thrust Tattle to the surface and nudged him over to a gravelbar at the edge of the creek. Choking and half drowned, the dog struggled to rise. Failing, it tremblingly crawled away on its belly.

Swimmer turned and tried to follow Ripple upstream, but made poor progress until she returned and helped him. They made a game of it, and suddenly it was great fun just to be alive and able to battle the current, and, for a little while, the fact of a broken leg didn't matter in the least.

But as they finally surfaced at the flat rock near the den, all the threat of man's world could be felt again, stronger than ever.

An anxious Penny was waiting on the rock.

"What happened?" she asked quickly. "I heard Tattle barking, then he made an awful sound . . ."

"Aw, we had to give the scumpy weasel a ducking," Swimmer admitted. "He wouldn't shut up. But I don't think he'll bother us for a while now."

"Oh, dear, I hope not. I haven't much time. Come close and I'll try to cut off that harness." As she spoke she took pliers and a hacksaw from the same bag she had used yesterday and went determinedly to work on one of the shoulder links. "Keep watch, everybody," she panted. "Scruff's not with me, and Mr. Sykes is liable to be down here any minute. We just can't let him catch us."

Presently she paused a moment and gasped, "Golly, I didn't know silver was so hard to cut! Looks like I'll never get it apart." She went back to work, and added, "Weaver and his pa are making a big dip net to catch you—I mean they think they can catch you with it, only they don't know anything about otters. Mr. Sykes is so excited over the reward he's about to bust a seam. Is it really two thousand dollars?"

"It's twenty thousand," Swimmer said gloomily.

"*Twenty* thousand!" she gasped. "But—but—I can't believe—"

"Aw, fiffle, what's twenty thousand? Don't you think I'm worth more?"

"But of course you are! If you want to look at it that way, I mean. Only I can't. There's something so scary and awful about money, and the way it can make nice things ugly. Was it Mr. Green—Clarence—who told you about the reward?"

"Yes, and he should have been back hours ago. Have you seen him?"

Penny almost dropped the saw. "You—you mean he hasn't been here all day?"

"No, ding blatt it." Swimmer's voice was a dismal croak. "Something's happened."

She sawed in silence for a while. Then, "Do—do you s'pose he's in trouble 'cause he's black?"

"Huh? What difference does that make?"

"Well, some folks up here don't like black people. I've known lots of black people—well, seven or eight, anyway —and I thought they were nice. But Mr. Sykes hates them."

"Anybody that could hate Clarence is a—a skrink and a blatthead," Swimmer said emphatically.

He was about to remark that most of the human tribe, from the way they acted, didn't seem to have frog sense. But before he could voice his opinion, several things happened almost at once.

First, with a little cry of relief, Penny managed to cut through the link. It released the loop of chain about his neck, and she immediately began tugging at the rest of the harness, trying to pull it back over his body. He was struggling to get out of it when he felt a sharp twinge of uneasiness and became aware of warnings from both Willow and Ripple.

"Somebody's coming!" he gasped and struggled frantically to free himself. The harness came off, and Penny, at the sudden sound of voices, snatched it up and flung it as far as she could into the tangle on the other side of the tree.

It had been Swimmer's intention to carry the bell and harness far back into the den, where no one would be likely to find it, but it was too late for that now. He dove and followed Willow and Ripple into their hiding place. A few seconds later he was at his post in the limb, watching Weaver Sykes and his father approach.

In Weaver's hands, in place of his gun, were a pitchfork and a slender pole. Grady Sykes carried a large, crudely fashioned dip net made of a sapling split at the end to spread a few feet of chicken wire. He was lean like Weaver, but with a grim, square face and a twisted slit of a mouth that drooped on one side. This lower corner of his mouth was stained with tobacco juice that had dripped down to the front of his overalls.

The two paused under the tree, arguing over the best place to begin the search, and the proper way of netting a tomfool otter with a silver bell around its neck. Swimmer, peering down at the net, wondered if they expected him to be accommodating enough to crawl into the silly thing, or perhaps allow himself to be stabbed and held by the pitchfork.

Grady Sykes stepped farther around the tree, and saw Penny for the first time. He spat angrily.

"Ain't I done told you to stay away from down here?"

"B-but I just wanted to watch—"

"You git back to the house! Wait—what you got in that bag?"

"It—it's just some things I—"

With his free hand Grady Sykes snatched the paper bag from her. He tried to shake it open, failed, then turned it over and shook its contents on the ground.

Suddenly he swore. "So *you*'re the one took my pliers! An' the hacksaw! What d'you think you're doin' down here with them tools?"

Penny swallowed. When she failed to speak, he dropped the net and seized her by the shoulder. His other hand swung back to strike. "You're up to something no good. What is it, girl? Answer me, dang blast you!"

Swimmer didn't see Clarence approach, or even hear him. But all at once Clarence was there, complete with hiking staff, knapsack, sleeping bag, and a familiar cloth sack that had always been used for carrying tinned fish.

"Hold it!" Clarence ordered quietly. "Don't you hit that girl."

Grady Sykes jerked around. He took one look at Clarence, and his jaws knotted. He spat again.

"I don't allow your kind around here. Git your danged self off'n my property!"

"This is not your property," Clarence said patiently. "It happens to be a wildlife refuge area, and I have a permit to be on it. Have you?"

The reply infuriated Grady Sykes. "I done told you to git off," he said dangerously. "An' I ain't takin' no more back talk off'n you." Abruptly he grabbed the pitchfork from Weaver and swung it hard at Clarence. *Now move!*"

Clarence moved. But all he did was drop the bag and bring the hiking staff up to a bayonet defense position. To Swimmer it was evident that Clarence was a past master at this sort of thing and probably had taught it to countless recruits. Two quick taps and the pitchfork was sent flying into the forest.

Any further trouble was interrupted by the short baying of a hound upstream. Following it came a shout, and the muffled sound of men's voices in the distance.

The hound appeared first. It was straining at a leash, the end of which was held by a tall, shambling man in a dirty, brown jacket and mud-stained boots.

The dog was new—a different beast entirely than the one he remembered. But the man was the same.

At the first hated sight and scent of the man, even before he saw the snake-cold eyes in the swarthy face, Swimmer felt the shock of awful recognition.

Below, hired to come and catch him once again, was the trapper who had killed his mother and sold his sister and himself to Dr. Hoffman.

6

He Is in a Spot

At the sight of his enemy, the human creature he hated more than anything on earth, Swimmer's lips drew back in a snarl. He trembled. The trembling began in hate but ended in a sudden feeling of helplessness that slowly turned to fear.

Nothing would ever wipe out the hate, but he had no thought of revenge. The way things were, revenge was impossible. He would be lucky, in fact, if the den was not discovered. Tattle had suspected it, and Clarence had guessed it right away. If Snake Eyes found it—he never thought of the trapper by any other name—Willow and Ripple would be in mortal danger.

Below him Grady Sykes had turned his back on Clarence and was directing his anger at Snake Eyes. He cursed and spat out, "If it's that fool otter you're after, just keep agoin'! This here's private property. I aim to do all the otter-catching done around here!"

"You aimin' to do it with that?" The trapper growled and kicked contemptuously at the chicken wire net. "Don't bug me, mister. Save it for Mr. Tippet."

In sudden surprise, Clarence exclaimed, "Don't tell me Mr. Tippet is here!"

"He's here," the trapper muttered in his grating voice. "Right behind me somewhere." He looked hard at Clarence and rubbed grimy knuckles over an unshaven jaw. "Who d'ya think you are?"

"I'm Clarence Green. I've been taking care of Swimmer ever since Doc Hoffman got him."

"I'll be jugged!" Then, suspiciously, "I don't figger this. How come you happened to git here ahead o' me an' my dog?"

Before Clarence could explain, Mr. Tippet and two other men came into view. One, roughly dressed and burdened with a heavy pack, was obviously the trapper's helper. The other, who carried a camera, had the familiar look of a newsman. But it was upon the elegant and self-important little Mr. Tippet that Swimmer turned his unhappy attention.

At the first mention of Mr. Tippet's name, his sinking spirits had taken a sharper tumble. Mr. Tippet was Doc Hoffman's front man. And wherever the front man was to be seen, it was a safe bet that old Doc himself wasn't very far away.

As he reached the tree, Mr. Tippet, a living picture of what the well-dressed man should wear in the woods, quickly unlimbered a walkie-talkie he was carrying and went straight to the trapper.

"What's the score, Jules?" he demanded. His edged voice was sharper than usual, for he was out of breath. Swimmer knew he detested the woods and everything in it. "Have you found him yet? Is he here?"

"He's here somewhere," Snake Eyes answered. "I ain't found him yet, but I will. He ain't apt to go much farther."

"You're sure of that? What's to keep him from going on downstream?"

"Pshaw, he's come this far only because he's lookin' for food an' a place to hide. He ain't doin' no more travelin' with a bad leg."

"Good Lord, is he injured?"

"I thought the critter was from the first. Now I've found enough sign to be sure of it. I think he's got a busted leg."

"Oh, dear me!" Mr. Tippet exclaimed and brought the walkie-talkie closer to his face. "A broken leg! Did you hear that, Dr. Hoffman?"

"I heard it," came the slightly muffled but all-too-familiar voice from the speaker. "Tippet, ask Jules if there's a chance of locating Swimmer before dark."

"I ain't sure," growled Snake Eyes. "It depends on how far down the creek the critter went before he found himself a hole. There's a heap o' holes around here. A smart critter like that, he's liable to come all the way back—"

He was suddenly interrupted by Penny, who had been standing silently to one side ever since the arrival of Clarence, nervously biting her lip. "There—there's a beaver pond downstream," she said brightly. "If—if Swimmer's lame, wouldn't he go to a place like that? I mean, it would be so easy for him to catch frogs and things there . . ."

"Mebbe," the trapper muttered. "We'll look it over." He turned to the straining hound, a huge black ungainly beast of uncertain mixtures, and clicked his tongue. "Go find 'im, Devil!"

It was only now, as the trapper and his helper were hurrying away, that Mr. Tippet became aware of Clarence for the first time.

He stared and abruptly burst out, "My word! How did you get here? You'd better explain yourself, Clarence!"

Clarence said politely, "I sort of followed my nose here, Mr. Tippet."

"Followed your nose? Nonsense! You're not a hound!"

"Oh, the Forest Service helped me, sir. And I spent some time studying the creeks. This seemed the most likely area. Trouble is, sir, that the gentleman yonder, Mr. Sykes—he has the trout farm you probably saw on the road—feels that we're trespassing—"

"You're danged right you're trespassing!" Grady Sykes sputtered wrathfully. "An' if that fool varmint's found around here, I'm claiming part of the reward."

"I've never heard such drivel!" Mr. Tippet snapped, eyeing him sternly. "My good man, I happen to have a map that shows all this land along the creek to be part of a wildlife refuge area. I find it very strange that you would pretend to claim it. You'd better tell me why."

There was a moment's silence. Suddenly Penny, white-faced but defiant, cried, "I'll tell you why! It—it's because he hates otters, and—and he's got traps set all over the place!"

"Traps?" Mr. Tippet echoed.

"Traps!" said Clarence hoarsely. "Good Lord!"

"Danged varmints!" Grady Sykes muttered. "That's all them otters are. A man's got a right . . ." All at once, with a baleful look at Penny, he snatched up a stick and started toward her. "I'll learn you to watch your tongue, you worthless, no-account . . ."

As Penny darted away, the newsman, who had silently been taking pictures all the while, quickly turned his camera upon them. Penny dodged behind Clarence, and Grady Sykes stopped abruptly. At the same moment a blast of sound came from Mr. Tippet's walkie-talkie.

"*Traps!*" roared that famous voice. "Do something, Tippet! Get rid of the things! If Swimmer is harmed in any way

64

by a trap, I'll sue that rascal for everything he's got. I'll wreck him! Do you hear me, Tippet?"

"I hear you, sir." Instantly Mr. Tippet pointed a stern finger at the owner of the trout farm. "And I trust *you* heard it, Sykes. Dr. Hoffman is not a man to be trifled with. If he says he'll wreck you, he will. I want all those traps accounted for. How many are there?"

Grady Sykes cursed. "That's my business!"

The newsman said, "Don't be a fool. If the game warden finds out about those traps, it'll cost you plenty. And I've just taken some pictures that won't make you look very good in court. How many traps did you set out around here?"

Penny said, "He had eight to start with."

"Then get them, Sykes," Mr. Tippet ordered. "And get them fast, or you'll learn what trouble is!"

Grady Sykes started grimly back up the creek, with Weaver shuffling angrily at his heels. Swimmer, watching them go, could feel the fury in them, and he was aware of Clarence's uneasiness.

Clarence said to Penny, "You were very brave to tell us what you did. But I hate to think how those people will act when you go home this evening."

"Oh, I'll tough it out, somehow. I always have. And Mrs. Sykes, she—she's not too bad. I mean, she licks me once in a while, but as long as I'm in the house she won't let the others do it."

"Humph!" Clarence grunted. "Such nice folks!" He glanced at Mr. Tippet and said quietly, "That was an awfully big reward Doc offered. It sort of threw everybody around here."

Mr. Tippet carefully switched off his walkie-talkie, and said, "I feel the reward was excessive, but Dr. Hoffman was terribly upset. He was beside himself, literally beside himself. In fact, Clarence, he was roaring—and I've never heard Dr. Hoffman roar before. The truth is, he thinks more of Swimmer than he does of anything on earth."

Up at his peephole Swimmer almost said "Phooey," but managed to control himself. The only thing old Doc really cared about was being the great Dr. Hoffman.

"So naturally," Mr. Tippet went on, "his first thought was to get as many people as possible out searching. Therefore the large reward. We had no idea Jules would be able to trail him so easily."

"Well, now that Swimmer's practically found," said Clarence, "don't you think it would be a good thing to cancel the reward? I mean, people are starting to swarm through the woods with everything from clubs to pitchforks. He's already hurt, and if some idiot happens to stumble over him before we do . . ."

"My word!" Mr. Tippet exclaimed. "I hadn't thought of that." He turned on the walkie-talkie and called, "Dr. Hoffman! Dr. Hoffman!"

It seemed to Swimmer that the chance to talk to Clarence, so he could find out what had happened, would never come. Impatiently he waited. While the traps were being located, Mr. Tippet and the newsman cruised back and forth along the creek, checking the progress made by Grady Sykes in one direction and Jules and his helper in the other. During a moment when they were alone at the tree, Penny told Clarence that she would try to slip down tomorrow after school. Then she hurried away to do her chores.

By twilight all but one of the traps had been found. It was too late to continue, and Mr. Tippet called a halt until morning. When the coast was finally clear, Swimmer crept out to the edge of the pebbly area, taking care not to step

66

from the water and leave a telltale scent. Clarence watchfully sat down on the rock beside him.

It was evident to Swimmer that Clarence was uneasy as well as upset. It added to his own uneasiness, which had been growing ever since the arrival of the trapper.

"Where's Snake Eyes?" he asked Clarence first.

"Who?"

"I mean that scumpy Jules. He worries me. Didn't you know that he's the one who caught me when I was little and —and killed my mother?"

"No! Good Lord!" Clarence was shocked. "I never saw the fellow before, though, of course, I've heard about him. He and his man are camping downstream a little way. I'll be on the watch for them."

Swimmer started to ask about the van, but Clarence suddenly peered at him closer in the fading light, and exclaimed softly, "Say, your bell's gone!"

"Sure is, praise be! And I don't miss it a bit." The moment he spoke he knew that wasn't quite true. He did miss the bell. Of course it was great not to have it there tinkling all the time and catching on things, but he'd become so used to the blatted nuisance that now he felt a little lost without it. And Ripple missed it too. She had loved it.

"How'd you get rid of it?" Clarence asked.

"Penny cut it with a hacksaw. That skrink of a Grady almost caught her at it—he found the hacksaw just before you came."

"I see."

"Clarence, can't we do something about her?"

"I'd like to. An idea has been buzzing around in my head, but I'm not sure what I can arrange. Right now we're all in a spot."

"What's happened?"

"Swimmer, if I don't get you away from here tonight, you're going to be caught. Don't you realize that?"

Swimmer shivered in the chill air drifting down the creek. He hated to admit it, but Clarence could be right. Until a few hours ago he'd thought the den was safe. But no longer. Not with Snake Eyes here, and that big black glump of a dog. If that dog was any good at all, he'd sniff out the tree in the morning. Then Snake Eyes would go to work.

He had tried to forget that awful day when Snake Eyes had caught him, but suddenly it all came back again: the horror of the choking gas that had been forced into their den, the panic, and the blind scramble to get outside to air. Only, there'd been the big bag net over the entrance, and no way to escape it.

"Clarence," he began, "I'm not going anywhere without Willow and Ripple. If I can talk 'em into going up to the van, will you take us to another creek?"

Clarence sighed. "That's what I'd hoped to do. But I can't do it tonight. We'll have to think of something else."

"What's wrong?" Swimmer asked. "Did the van break down?"

"You're so right," said Clarence, nodding. "Everything seemed okay when I got back to it this morning, but I'd hardly left the bridge behind when I hit a rough spot in the road, and the front axle broke. I think it was already cracked from that jolting we took the other night when we missed the landslide, so all it needed was a final bump."

Clarence sighed again. "Anyway, there I was. Ten miles from town on a back road in the mountains on a Sunday morning. I'm the wrong color to expect a ride from anybody, so I started to hoof it. But I hadn't gone a half mile when a fellow stopped and picked me up. Swimmer, you'd never guess who he was."

"An—an Indian?" Swimmer offered, cocking his head to one side.

"You read my mind!"

"Aw, fiffle. Even a frog can do that."

Clarence spread his hands. "We ought to go in business together. Like you said, he was an Indian. A Cherokee—their reservation is just over the mountain yonder. A little old man he was, with a face like a dried apple. He'd been in the Army too, and we hit it up just right. Name's Owl. Mr. Hiram Owl. If it hadn't been for him, I wouldn't be here now. On Sunday everything's closed, but he got a man to come out with a wrecker and haul the van in to a garage. Tomorrow they'll start working on it."

Clarence paused and shook his head. "So you see, we're in a spot. It may be a couple days or more before we have any transportation. We can't wait that long."

Swimmer pondered his predicament. Alone, it wouldn't be any superfeat to get clean away, even with a bum leg. Without the bell and harness to worry him, he could make it easily to the next creek. All he needed was for Clarence to carry him over the next ridge, so he wouldn't leave a trail leading away from here.

But Clarence couldn't carry them all. And he doubted if Willow would allow anyone but Penny to touch her, even if she were willing to leave. This was Willow's own den on her favorite creek, and if she went anywhere, it would be down-stream in water that she knew.

It was a problem.

Suddenly he asked, "Clarence, what's the creek like between here and the bridge?"

"Rough," came the answer. "There are some fine pools, but there are a lot of mean spots you'd have to walk around even if you were in top swimming condition. And wherever you put foot to ground and leave a scent . . ." Clarence shook his head. "And that's not all. I'll bet every kid in the country, and his old man, is out trying to spot you."

"Aw, blatts! Without the van we really are stuck. Guess we'll have to take it the way Penny does—just tough it out somehow. But maybe I can fool Snake Eyes."

"Yeah? How?"

"Our place has another entrance. Let me do a little figuring, and I'll come up with something."

"It better be good!"

"It will be. You—you're going in town in the morning? With Mr. Owl?"

Clarence whistled softly. "I can't keep anything from you, can I?"

"Not much. You two have got something cooking."

Clarence nodded. "We have, but I'd rather not talk about it yet. Sometimes it's bad luck to talk about schemes until you're ready to jump. But I will tell you a mighty interesting thing about Mr. Owl. He's a lawyer."

"Is that good?"

"You can bet your webbed feet it's good! Having that van break down when it did could be about the best thing that ever happened—if you can just keep from being caught for a while. Are you sure you can manage it?"

"Sure enough. But like people say, Clarence, only two things are really sure in this vale of tears. Anyway, in a pinch, we'll leave the tree and swim down to the beaver pond. We can hide out in one of their dens."

"They're called lodges."

"Aw, fiffle, it's all the same. We ought to be safe there for a while."

"Until that fellow Jules cuts the dam and drains the pond," Clarence muttered. "And don't think he won't if he

70

learns you're there. And he couldn't care less that this is a wildlife refuge area. H'mm. That gives me an idea. I'll tell Mr. Owl about it and see what he thinks. I've told him all about you, Swimmer. He's mighty interested in meeting you—"

"Watch it!" Swimmer's warning was a froglike croak as he caught the hound scent, suddenly strong. He had been aware of it all the time without thinking about it, just as he had been aware of other scents and many sounds in the early dark. They had told him of the family of skunks living under the bank not many yards away, and of the flying squirrels that had left their hollow high overhead to play in the night, and of the presence of a dozen other creatures near and far. But the scent of the trapper's dog was all at once much too close.

Swimmer settled down against the rock so that only his face was above the water. A coldness and a hardness came over him. His lips drew back, and his feet dug into the pebbles for a firmer grip.

The big dog suddenly appeared, a black shape against the shadowed rocks. It gave a low growl as it neared Clarence, but Clarence did not move. He spoke to it sharply and ordered it away. Instead, the hound snarled and sprang down to the pebbly area, barking furiously.

Hate flooded Swimmer. Had he been alone he would have attacked the dog on the instant and taken his chances on pulling it into the water, even though it outweighed him by many pounds. But too much was at stake tonight. He must get the hound into the creek and jerk it under, before Snake Eyes came. And this time he would kill. If he didn't, it might cost Willow and Ripple their lives.

He waited, every muscle tense. Still barking, the hound reached the water's edge. Swimmer drew a deep breath, taking in enough air to last him nearly five minutes in a struggle. He prepared to spring. But almost instantly, as if realizing his danger, the beast retreated.

Without a sound to announce his approach, the dark curved shape of the hound's master loomed above the rocks. The beam of a flashlight played over the swirling surface of the stream. Swimmer submerged completely. Seconds later he came up in the safety of the tangled roots immediately behind Clarence.

"You was sittin' right here all the time," the trapper was saying in his grating voice. "Sittin' right here, an' you didn't see nothin'?"

"I was enjoying the night," Clarence said mildly. "Until your dog came."

Snake Eyes cursed. "There's something mighty queer about you! Once my dog's on a scent, he don't never let go. The way he barked, that otter was right here close."

"Well?" said Clarence.

"I bet you know where he is! If you do, you dang sure better tell me!"

"If I knew, Mr. Jules, you're the last man I'd ever tell."

There was a moment of dangerous silence. At last Snake Eyes ground out, "I got a mind to break your ugly neck."

"I wouldn't advise you to try it, Mr. Jules. I spent more than twenty years in the Army teaching men how to break other men's necks, and how to do all sorts of other unpleasant things. But if you want me to prove it to you, I'll be glad to oblige."

Snake Eyes cursed again, muttered some threats, growled an order to his dog, and turned away.

Swimmer waited until his senses told him the danger had passed, then he swam back to his former place.

"Drat that Snake Eyes!" he grumbled. "He came too soon. I was all ready to take that dirty glump of hound."

"Swimmer, are you out of your mind? You couldn't handle a dog that size—not with a broken leg!"

"Phooey! I could handle one twice that size in the water. And my leg's doing fine; I hardly feel it now. I sure wish I'd taken that dirty glump. I've got an awful feeling about him . . ."

"Well, forget about him for tonight. How about a can of tuna fish to help you go to sleep?"

"Huh? Tuna fish? Say, have you got another can with you?"

"Sure thing."

"Well, open them up, because I want you to meet a friend of mine. Clarence, she's really something! I mean, she may be sort of young, but she's cute as a water bug and smart as they come. Why, I'll bet it wouldn't take any time for her to learn to talk as well as I do."

"Well, I declare!" said Clarence. "I'd sure like to meet her."

Swimmer made a quick trip through the tunnel, and returned presently with Ripple. She stood up timidly beside him, and held out her small webbed "hands" to touch Clarence's fingers as she was introduced.

Swimmer said, "Wouldn't we make a pair onstage, Clarence? I mean, if each of us wore a silver bell, and answered questions together. See? What d'you think, Clarence?"

Clarence shook his head. "I—I just don't have words for it, Swimmer."

73

7

He Speaks to Mr. Tippet

A sleepy chickadee, somewhere in the tangle high above him, was trying to announce the dawn when Swimmer climbed to his post in the hollow limb. Below in the vague light Clarence was swiftly rolling up his sleeping bag, preparing to leave.

When he was ready, Clarence glanced up and whispered, "Are you there, old pal?"

"Right here," said Swimmer.

"I've got an awful lot to do," Clarence told him, "but I'll be back just as soon as possible. This is going to be a day."

Swimmer had the unpleasant feeling that this was going to be a whumping whale of a day, and he wasn't exactly looking forward to it. But all he said was, "If I'm not here, you'll know that we've all gone down to the beaver pond."

He watched Clarence fade silently into the blackness of the slope, then he turned his attention downstream. The place where Snake Eyes had camped was far beyond his range of vision, but he knew that the trapper and his helper were up. A faint smell of coffee was coming from that direction.

Suddenly he heard the muttering of the hound. It was in

the distance at first but swiftly drew nearer until he saw it directly below, a dark threatening shape with its nose to the ground, weaving on the old scent, undecided. It paused and glared up at the tree, and instinctively Swimmer turned his attention away from it lest the beast become aware of him. Almost angrily the dog sniffed the ground again, then raced around the tree and disappeared upstream.

Now Snake Eyes and his helper came into view. They stopped and stood listening, evidently waiting on the hound. The helper said, "That black feller's gone. Wonder what he's up to?"

"I dunno, an' I don't care," Snake Eyes growled. "He jest better stay shut of me." He raised his voice and called, "Find 'im, Devil!"

The hound came back, nose to the ground and sure of itself now. Swinging around the tree, it went down to the pebbly area at the water's edge and began to bay.

"I knowed it," Snake Eyes growled. "He seen the critter last night, right there. Git your stick, Jake, an' poke around in them roots yonder. Could be a hole back under 'em."

Swimmer's none-too-high spirits began to spiral downward as Jake, clad in hip boots, entered the water and waded around the rocks to the base of the tree. Using a long, green stick, he began prodding between the roots.

Jake found the opening, but when his stick touched the granite obstruction around which the passageway curved, he shook his head. "Ain't nothin' here."

Snake Eyes swore. "It's got to be close by. There's a heap o' holes around, so start workin' downstream an' I'll work up."

The day gradually brightened. Presently the sun climbed above the eastern ridge and bright shafts of light streamed through the crowding trees.

By the timekeeping portion of Swimmer's brain, it was

exactly nine o'clock when matters took a turn for the worse and things began to happen. First, from somewhere on the other side of the tree, he heard a small, timid voice calling his name.

"Swimmer? Oh, Swimmer, where are you?"

It was Penny, and she didn't sound quite like herself. Snake Eyes and Jake were both working on the other side of the creek at the moment, so he called as softly as he could with his gnome voice, "Right here, Penny. Over your head."

Penny, closely followed by a watchful Scruff, came into view. She glanced up, and now he saw that both sides of her face were discolored by bruises.

"Hey, what's happened to you?" he asked. "I thought you'd be in school today."

"I—I didn't really want to go," she said. "So I laid out."

"Huh? Laid out?"

"That's what the kids at my school say when they skip class. Everything around here is so—so upset and all, that when I saw the school bus coming I just couldn't get on it. And I hated for people to see me, 'cause I look so awful. Mr. Sykes caught me last night and bopped me, and I—"

"The dirty skrink! Where—"

"It happened in the house, where I didn't think it would," she hastened to explain. "And somehow Scruff knew it—and though I'd told him never to come near the place, he came anyway and made a terrible fuss at the door like he was going to break in. Golly, he sure scared everybody! But he was smart enough to leave before they could shoot him. First thing this morning Mr. Sykes and Weaver got their guns and went out to hunt him. They're still scared, they don't know whether he's just a wild dog or—or something worse . . ."

She gave a small giggle and added, "But as I was saying,

76

with everything the way it is, I just couldn't go to school today. So I went and found Scruff, then I thought I'd better have a look at Clarence's van, just in case we had to hide in it later. Only, the van isn't where he said he'd leave it, and —and I can't even find Clarence. Is—is something wrong?"

"Looks like everything's wrong," Swimmer grumbled. "The van's in the garage with a broken axle, and Clarence has gone to town with Mr. Owl, that Indian lawyer. Don't ask me why. And here I am up a tree, practically trapped— You'd better hide! I hear Mr. Tippet coming."

"Oh, I don't mind Mr. Tippet, but maybe I'd better get Scruff out of sight, just in case."

As she turned away her lip trembled, and she dabbed at one swollen eye with the back of her hand. "I—I don't see why things have to be the way they are," she said almost plaintively. "Wouldn't it be wonderful if we could all go off somewhere? I mean, just you and me and Clarence and Scruff and Willow and Ripple and—and—"

"That's a whumptious idea," Swimmer admitted, and mentally added Miss Primm to the list, as well as the mynah bird and the white mouse. He was beginning to miss all three of them.

It was at this moment, when he realized how he felt and considered what Penny had said, that the seed of a brilliant plan began to sprout in the back of his head.

Swimmer was so taken with his plan that he failed to see Penny leave and was only barely aware that Snake Eyes had crossed back to this side of the creek, and was approaching to meet Mr. Tippet.

"Well, Jules," he heard Mr. Tippet say sharply, "what's the score this morning?"

"We kinda narrowed it down," Snake Eyes growled.

"That critter ain't a hundred feet from where we're standing. More likely fifty. My dog Devil seen 'im last night, right yonder in the water."

"You're sure of that?"

"I know Devil. When he acts a certain way, he's seein' what he's after."

"Then why can't you find him?" Mr. Tippet demanded. "What's the delay?"

Snake Eyes spat. "Either he's in a skunk hole under the bank yonder, or he's in a den somewhere under this tree. That skunk hole's got skunks in it. Gittin' 'im out's gonna be a problem."

"Swimmer wouldn't crawl in with skunks, would he?" said Mr. Tippet, aghast.

Snake Eyes spat again. "Might. But it's just as big a problem if he's denned up under the tree with a family of otters, which I kinda figger he is."

"I fail to understand you, Jules."

"Pshaw. When I find the right spot, an' stake a net over the entrance, I'll gas the critters out. But when a heap of 'em hit the net at the same time, like they will, I won't be able to handle 'em—unless I quiet 'em fast with a club."

"Jules, this is a wildlife sanctuary. It's against the law to kill anything here."

Snake Eyes spat for the third time and turned away in disgust. "I don't pay no mind to the law. You want that fool critter caught, I'll have to do it my way." He nodded to the waiting Jake and muttered, "Let's have another look at them roots. I got a feelin' we missed something."

Swimmer almost groaned when he saw the two men wade into the creek and begin probing about the root tangle again. This time he had no doubt whatever that the entrance would be found. But how soon? It was almost too much to hope that he could stick it out here till Clarence returned, but he was resolved to stay as long as possible and not leave the tree until the last possible moment. When that moment came, Ripple and her mother knew exactly what to do. They would hurry into the side tunnel, and he would follow and try to close it behind him with dirt and stones. After that he'd have to sort of play it by ear. With any sort of luck they might be able to return to their den and forget the beaver pond.

Below him Mr. Tippet unlimbered his walkie-talkie and made contact with Dr. Hoffman.

"We have it narrowed down, Doctor, There are some, ah, difficulties, but I think everything will be under control by noon."

"See that it is, Tippet," came that well-known voice from some unknown quarter, possibly a motel room. "I want this thing settled. Let me speak to Clarence."

"Sir, Clarence isn't here. I haven't seen him since last evening. He told me he was going to camp here last night, but when I returned this morning there was no sign of him."

"Confound him! He's been acting very strangely ever since Swimmer ran away."

"Indeed, he has, sir! And he'll have some explaining to do— Pardon me, sir, but here comes that fellow Sykes from the trout farm."

Raising his voice, Mr. Tippet demanded, "Sykes, what about that last trap? Have you found it yet?"

Grady Sykes, shotgun in hand, swung into view under the tree. Close behind him, limping a little, came Tattle.

"Dang the trap!" Grady Sykes spat out. "I ain't got no time to fool with that now. There's a big varmint of a wild dog on the loose. He tried to break in my house last night!"

"What's this?" exclaimed Mr. Tippet. "A wild dog? Why, I've never heard of such a thing!"

"We got 'em in these mountains," Grady Sykes told him.

"They're worse'n wolves. This un's the biggest an' the meanest I ever seen. Came right up on the porch an' tried to bust down the door!"

Both Snake Eyes and his helper stopped their search and climbed up on the bank. "You say a wild dog tried to bust in your house last night?" Snake Eyes shook his head in disbelief.

"But that's exactly what happened!" Grady Sykes insisted. "My whole family seen it."

"What'd he look like?"

"Just like a big yeller wolf. He slammed agin the door, snarling an' carrying on something terrible. Plum' mad he was!"

"Was he frothing at the mouth?"

"Sure, he was frothing! The porch light was on, an' I seen 'im plain as day from the side window. I run an' got my gun, an' fore I could even raise it he took off like a flash an' was gone."

"Then he warn't mad," said Snake Eyes. "He was just smart."

"If he warn't mad, he was sure tetched or had a worm in the brain! I never seen a varmint carry on an' act so killing mean! I tell you—"

He was suddenly interrupted by a new voice that demanded, "Sykes, just what were you doing when that dog tried to break into the house?"

Swimmer's attention had been on Tattle, who was nosing suspiciously through the brush, and he had failed to notice the newsman approaching quietly from the rear. The newsman was a graying man with a protruding jaw and heavy shoulders. Swimmer remembered that yesterday Mr. Tippet had called him Mr. Hogarth, almost with respect.

"Dang it, I was minding my own business," Grady Sykes

80

spat out in answer to the newsman's question. "How come you—"

"Do you call it your business to beat a helpless girl so badly that she's ashamed to be seen in public?"

"Who says I beat her?"

"*I* say it!" Mr. Hogarth's jaw went forward a little farther. "I've pictures I took yesterday to prove it. I've another I took this morning that explains the dog. Shall I tell you why that dog tried to break in last night?"

"No, blast you! Just because you bought the paper in town, you needn't think you can stick your danged nose in everybody's business. You mess with me—"

"You bloody fool, don't you realize that dog was trying to protect Penny last night? He's her friend. If you ever put a finger on her again and he catches you at it . . ."

Grady Sykes paled. Slowly, with the back of his hand, he wiped tobacco juice from the corner of his mouth. His lips moved soundlessly as he fumbled for words.

In the sudden silence the only sound was a sharp bark from Tattle, who was tugging at something bright in the bushes. Swimmer saw what it was on the instant. In despair he watched the brown mongrel drag the object across the ground and drop it at his master's feet.

Grady Sykes picked it up and stared at it. Abruptly Mr. Tippet snatched it from him.

"Why—why—my word! This is Swimmer's bell and harness!"

The newsman came closer and touched the dangling end of the chain. "Odd," he murmured. "Looks like it's been cut."

"Yeah," growled Snake Eyes, extending a grimy paw to the harness. "It's been cut. With a hacksaw."

"With a hacksaw!" Grady Sykes cried hoarsely. With

both hands he grabbed the harness from Mr. Tippet and held it up. His face darkened and the silver bell tinkled as his hands began to shake. He cursed. "I knowed she was up to something when I caught her with that hacksaw. She found that danged varmint—an' she let 'im go! *She let 'im go!* Throwed all that reward money away!"

He cursed again and hurled the harness to the ground. "When I git my hands on that worthless girl—"

"You touch Penny again," Mr. Hogarth warned, "and you're going to get killed."

Swimmer's uneasy eyes swung back to Tattle. The brown dog had trotted to the base of the tree. It looked up at him knowingly and suddenly began to shatter the morning with its sharp triumphant yapping.

Instantly Grady Sykes jerked around. A corner of his twisted mouth curled upward. "By jingo!" he cried. "Tattle's found the varmint! He's holed up in the tree. I'm gonna cut that danged tree down!"

"You ain't cuttin' nothin' down," Snake Eyes told him. "I know where the critter is—I trailed 'im here. I been hired to catch the critter, an' I aim to do it, but I don't aim to have you around gittin' in my way. Y'hear?"

From somewhere in the distance, faintly, Swimmer became aware of Weaver's voice calling, "Pa! Where are you? Pa! The bank wants you to phone 'em right away. It's important!"

Grady Sykes seemed to freeze. Then slowly he turned and started back up the creek trail. With every step he moved a little faster until finally he was running.

The idea that had sprouted in the back of Swimmer's ever-restless brain was still growing in spite of unpleasant interruptions and the uncertainties of the moment.

Occasionally he allowed it to come forward for a quick study, then back it went to sizzle some more on a rear burner. Just how it might fit in with the idea in the back of Clarence's mind he wasn't quite sure. He wasn't sure, in fact, just what *was* in the back of Clarence's mind, for Clarence himself had been a little hazy about it when he left. But there'd been a glimpse of several ingredients, of which the main ones were Mr. Owl and Clarence's savings through the years. Then there was the bank.

Because the bank was an ingredient, Swimmer had watched the departure of Grady Sykes with considerable interest. Now it gave him momentary satisfaction to watch Snake Eyes drive the yapping Tattle away before going back into the creek to continue the search. Over by the boulders, camera ready for any possible action, Mr. Hogarth was talking to Mr. Tippet about Penny.

"You see," the newsman was saying, "I'd parked my car up there at the end of a logging road and taken a shortcut down here, or I never would have run into her. First thing I knew I heard a growl. I thought it was a bear, then I saw this big rascal of a dog ready to tear me apart. Behind him was Penny, sitting on a rock, looking like the world had come to an end. Her face was a mess, both eyes nearly swollen shut . . .

"Anyway, when she gave the word, that dog allowed me to come up and talk to her. So I got the whole story."

"It's shocking," said Mr. Tippet. "Utterly shocking. I'm surprised that Welfare doesn't do something about her."

"Welfare!" Mr. Hogarth snorted. "Grady Sykes has a sister that practically runs the Welfare office. Regular battle-ax. That's how he got the girl. Just wanted her for a slavey."

"But can't something—"

"There's little that can be done except to adopt her, and

no one around here will do that. I couldn't, even if I were willing—I'm a bachelor and live at the hotel. Anyway, the girl would rather stay here than leave her friends."

"Eh? What friends, Mr. Hogarth?"

"Her wild friends, Mr. Tippet. That monster of a dog for one, he's as wild as a wolf. And, judging from the things she let slip, about every wild creature around here, including all the otters."

"But—but—that's incredible!" Mr. Tippet exclaimed.

"She's an incredible person," said Mr. Hogarth. "The most remarkable I've ever known, as I'm only now finding out. Of course, when I talked to her this morning, I didn't even dream that she'd already found Swimmer and had probably been taking care of him. Why, I'll bet she'd just finished cutting off that bell and harness when we came down here yesterday!"

"My word! She must have."

"The thing would be a nuisance to an animal in the wild state," Mr. Hogarth went on. Suddenly he chuckled. "And there she was, knowing all the time where Swimmer was hiding and not letting out a peep. Even sent Jules down to the beaver pond. What a girl!"

Mr. Tippet glanced at his watch and reached over and made an adjustment on the walkie-talkie standing with raised antenna on the rock between them. He was instantly rewarded by a rasp of static and a demanding voice.

"Tippet? Can you hear me, Tippet?"

"I hear you clearly, Doctor."

"Tippet, I've been monitoring your conversation. Just who is this incredible paragon of childhood who took it upon herself to remove Swimmer's bell and harness?"

"Her—her name is Penny, sir. She's a little redheaded orphan that the local Welfare office boarded out to that fellow Sykes."

84

"Then get her down there to help you. Impress it upon her that she had no business doing what she did. Swimmer is private property, and now it's her duty to help recover him if she knows where he is. Got that straight?"

Mr. Tippet looked uncomfortable. "I—I understand, Doctor. But—"

"No buts, Tippet. Get the girl down there. If she wants money, give it to her."

Mr. Hogarth leaned over and said, "Let me speak to him, Mr. Tippet."

"Doctor," said Mr. Tippet, "Mr. Hogarth, who owns the local paper here, would like a word with you."

"Go ahead, Hogarth," the renowned voice directed.

"It's just this, Dr. Hoffman. Penny happens to be on Swimmer's side, and nothing in the world could ever make her change her mind and help you."

"That's nonsense, Hogarth. You don't know people."

"I know this one," Mr. Hogarth retorted. "Furthermore, I've heard some of your lectures, and I've long been interested in Swimmer."

"Well?"

"Doctor," Mr. Hogarth continued, "you know better than anyone that Swimmer has a mind that is the equal of a human's and has the same range of feeling as a human."

"What's your point, Hogarth?"

"My point, Doctor, is that Swimmer had his reasons for running away. He'll hate you if you take him back by force and cage him again."

"Nonsense! He needs to be taught a lesson."

"Treat him that way and he'll refuse to work with you. Not only that, but it could be a very brutal business if Jules drives him out of his hiding place. We've reason to believe that more otters are with him, and they'll probably be killed."

85

"I can't help that."

"The devil you can't! This happens to be a wildlife sanctuary. If you allow any sort of outrage here, I'll give you some publicity you'll never get over."

"Don't threaten me with that one-horse paper of yours, Hogarth. I'm a man of means, and I'll wreck you!"

"Oh, no, Doctor. I'll wreck *you*. My one-horse paper is merely a hobby. I'm Johnson Hogarth, and my comments are printed in hundreds of papers and read by millions of Americans."

There was a shocked silence. At last Mr. Tippet gasped, "Good heavens, I'd been thinking you looked familiar, but I didn't realize you were *Johnson* Hogarth, the columnist!"

"Should it make so much difference? Am I a man or a name?" Mr. Hogarth shook his head. "We humans haven't much to be proud of. All I want is to make sure that Swimmer gets a fair deal—and that goes for all the other creatures."

Swimmer added Mr. Hogarth to his meager list of worthy humans and wondered what would really happen when the chips were down and Snake Eyes discovered the secret of the den's entrance. Not, of course, that he intended for Ripple and Willow and himself to remain there very long after that event. But Snake Eyes was tricky, and with the thought of Doc's money driving him on, he wouldn't let anything stand in his way—much less a little nastiness with a club.

Ever since the search had narrowed down to the tree, Swimmer's uneasiness had been growing. Now, all at once, he had the awful feeling that something was very wrong. It was so overwhelming that he left the peephole and crept down to the main part of the den.

In the dimness Willow and Ripple looked at him questioningly. *There is more trouble somewhere?*

There is a wrongness. I feel it. The other entrance— when did you use it last?

Before the ice melted, Willow told him. And Ripple added, *This entrance was frozen.*

Let us try the other entrance now.

Willow led the way. The tunnel was black and winding and suddenly so narrow from fallen rock that Swimmer stopped instinctively, then carefully backed out. In a moment Willow confirmed his fears. The rock walls had cracked and caved in, and the way was blocked completely. Nor could it be used as a temporary refuge, for there was no loose gravel or dirt available to seal it off tightly from the den.

Swimmer was shaken. Even his leg, which had not troubled him since Clarence left, began to throb again. What a blatthead I was! he thought. Why didn't we go to the beaver pond last night?

But it wasn't too late. If they worked it right, maybe they could slip past Snake Eyes and Jake and start downstream without being noticed.

He climbed hurriedly to his peephole to study the possibilities, and again his hopes fell. In the short time he had been away from his post, Snake Eyes had taken the precaution of stretching a fishnet entirely around the tangle of roots. Now, both trappers were leaning over the net, using long willow switches to probe the curving holes.

Even as Swimmer watched, Jake suddenly yelled as his flexible willow switch slid out of sight. "Found it! Trickiest thing I ever seen! I'll git the bag net."

It was now, for the first time in his life, that Swimmer prayed. It was not to the remote god of humans that he prayed, for he rather doubted that this divinity had much time for poor otters beset by humans. Instead, his appeal went to the Great Force he had been too young to understand when captured and too shut away from in the lab even to feel. But he had been aware of it from the very moment of escape. It was the Power that directs the flow of streams, that designs the spots for nests and dens, that gives the food and brings new days, that lives and speaks in every growing thing beneath the sun.

Please help us! he implored the Power.

And instantly, because he was thinking of Ripple and Willow instead of himself, the answer came. It was so simple that he wondered why he hadn't thought of it on his own, for even a one-eyed newt should have seen the straight of it.

Of course, it rather upset his plan. But maybe, somehow, the Power would help him there. . . .

Swimmer filled his lungs, pressed his face close against the opening, and called out as loudly and distinctly as he could in his smallish gnome voice:

"Mr. Tippet! Mr. Tippet! This is Swimmer in the tree. Hold everything! I'm ready to make a deal."

8

He Holds a Parley

On Mr. Tippet's strained and shattered face there was a curious mixture of shock and disbelief. On Mr. Hogarth's face there was only a great wonder. Snake Eyes, in the act of cutting himself a chew of tobacco while he waited in the water for Jake, dropped his plug and stared upward like a man rudely slapped. Jake, who had just climbed to the bank, became a temporary idiot, for he merely stood there blankly and shook his head.

It was Mr. Hogarth who first found his tongue. "Is that really you, Swimmer?"

"It's me, Mr. Hogarth. I'm almost over your head in this hollow place. And I'm mighty glad you're here and on my side. Please, tell Mr. Tippet to tell Snake Eyes—Jules, I mean—to take the net away from the tree. They've no right to bother my friends. I'm the one they're after."

Mr. Tippet gasped, "What—what is this? Some kind of a joke?"

Mr. Hogarth said, "It's no joke, Mr. Tippet. I can just make out Swimmer's face up there in that hole between the leaves. He knows how to talk."

"But—but that's impossible!"

"Oh, come now! I once knew a dog that could talk, and I understand some dolphins are very proficient at it. Mr. Tippet, Swimmer made a request. What are you going to do about it?"

"Oh, devil take it! Swimmer, what's this all about?"

"I told you I was ready to make a deal, Mr. Tippet. Tell that Jules to take his net away first and go back to where he has his dog tied up. I—I've got friends here with me and I don't want him anywhere around."

Mr. Tippet shook his head, a little dazed. "But Swimmer, he—he's not going to hurt your friends. He's been expressly warned not to."

"Phooey!" Swimmer cried. "I know what's in his scumpy mind better than you! He's all set to gas the tree and kill my friends when they come out—and then say he couldn't help it. He wants their pelts!"

"Swimmer, you—you don't know what you're talking about."

"I do too! He's a dirty snake-eyed skrink, and I say get rid of him! He's the one that trapped me years ago and killed my mother!"

Before the astounded Mr. Tippet could pull his wits together, Snake Eyes came sloshing out of the creek, cursing. His threats were drowned in the sudden blast that came from the walkie-talkie.

"Tippet! Confound it, Tippet, what the devil's going on there? Explain yourself!"

Mr. Hogarth, being much nearer, calmly picked up the walkie-talkie and said, "Doctor, this is Johnson Hogarth again. Mr. Tippet is having some trouble adjusting to an interesting new development. It may surprise you to know that Swimmer can talk. He is now trying to make a deal—"

"Talk? Talk? Swimmer has a high I.Q., but speech is beyond him. What nonsense is this?"

"It is not nonsense. Swimmer *can* talk, and he has a fine command of language, as four witnesses here can testify. Pardon me, but I see another development on the way. Here come Clarence and that Cherokee lawyer, Hiram Owl, and I believe that's a Wildlife Commission officer with them. H'mm. I'm afraid you're missing something by not being here, Doctor."

Swimmer was so glad to see Clarence's face again that he almost cried out, but caution held his tongue. Clarence was clearly up to something, and it had to do with the law. But what?

Below him Clarence spoke politely to Mr. Tippet and Mr. Hogarth and introduced Mr. Owl. The lawyer was a quiet, square-bodied little man with a brown-gold squarish face that did indeed look like a dried apple, as Clarence had said, for it was crossed with a thousand small wrinkles. It surprised Swimmer when the lawyer and Mr. Hogarth shook hands, smiling, and called each other by their first names.

"By the look in your eye, Hiram," said Mr. Hogarth, "you're ready to spring something. Another legal bomb?"

"Johnny," said Mr. Owl, "it's just a small token of my respect for the otter clan, of which I happen to be a member." He nodded toward the very blond young man in the khaki uniform and continued, "Gentlemen, this is Patrolman Swensen of the Wildlife Commission. Mr. Tippet, Patrolman Swensen is bringing you a restraining order from Judge Moffet's office."

"A restraining order?" Mr. Tippet said sharply. "To restrain me from doing what?"

"From doing what you're doing, sir," Patrolman Swensen said politely. He stepped forward and presented Mr. Tippet with a folded paper. "It's a new one to me, sir, but it's absolutely legal, for the judge explained it to me himself. It, er, forbids anyone to trap, catch, or in any manner to restrict the liberty of any wild, or formerly wild, creature indigenous to this area, while within the boundaries of a wildlife refuge."

"In other words," said Mr. Owl, "the law forbids you to touch Swimmer as long as he's here in the refuge."

Mr. Tippet stared at him, then glared accusingly at Clarence. Suddenly he snatched the walkie-talkie from Mr. Hogarth, and said hoarsely, "Doctor, this is Tippet. Were you able to hear enough to know what's happened here?"

"Yes, confound it, I heard it," Dr. Hoffman's voice roared back from the speaker. "Who is responsible for this —this infernal idiocy?"

Mr. Tippet leveled an accusing finger at Clarence, but before he could say anything the black man reached for the walkie-talkie and said politely, "Dr. Hoffman, this is Clarence. You can blame me for the restraining order, sir. I got it for Swimmer's own good. You see—"

"No, I don't see. I don't see at all! When I hired you I expected loyalty—"

"Sir, all my loyalty at this point is for Swimmer. If you'd just try to understand his side of it—"

"Clarence," Dr. Hoffman interrupted, and now his voice was like a grinding iceberg, "I'll have to remind you that Swimmer is a laboratory creature whose training has cost me a fortune. As such, he is my private property to do with as I wish, and he has no rights whatever."

This was too much for Swimmer. "Ding blatt it!" he shrieked. "I've got rights, same as anyone else! If you wouldn't act so skrinky, Doc, we might get along!"

There was an abrupt silence below. Every head jerked toward him. Patrolman Swensen's mouth gaped open, and he seemed powerless to close it. Mr. Owl's wise black eyes crinkled, and he smiled with a secret delight.

92

From the speaker Dr. Hoffman's voice demanded, "What the devil was that noise?"

Clarence said, "That was Swimmer, sir, and he insists that he does have rights."

Swimmer called, "Clarence, let me speak to him. I was all set to sell myself down the river when you came. Now, I don't have to, glory be! Maybe I can make a *real* deal!"

Clarence said worriedly, "If you can read my mind, Swimmer, you'll realize I wasn't able to buy very much on my shopping trip. Are you sure you know what you're doing now?"

Swimmer gulped. He saw clearly at last that Clarence had wanted to buy the mortgaged trout farm through the bank. Only, something had happened. Swimmer said, "Maybe we'd better let Mr. Owl handle this. I'm sorta shy on law-training, and Mr. Owl looks like my kind of man. Will you represent me, Mr. Owl?"

Mr. Owl's black eyes crinkled again. He smiled and nodded. "It would be a pleasure, Swimmer. Just tell me what you want done!"

"The net's the first thing," Swimmer said. "Tell the Wildlife officer to make that dirty trapper take it away. Then he can drive the scummy skrink and his rotty dog and his helper off the place. Ding 'em to dongnation, I never want to see 'em again!"

Swimmer drew a deep breath. The big deal was next. In spite of Clarence's failure at the bank, he was sure something could be arranged, and that Mr. Owl could work out the details. The main thing was to hold what people called a top-level conference. And the sooner, the better, for something told him that a delay might be dangerous. "Mr. Owl," he said, "tell Doc Hoffman that if he wants me to go on any more lecture tours with him, he'd better come out here right away and have a little talk."

By the timekeeping arrangement in the back of Swimmer's mind it was five minutes after three that afternoon when the great Dr. Rufus Hoffman, accompanied by Mr. Tippet who had gone to meet him at the road, came down through the forest to join the group under the beech tree. The trappers and the Wildlife man had left, and there remained only Clarence, Mr. Owl, and Mr. Hogarth.

Dr. Hoffman had been anything but pleased with the idea of the meeting, and Swimmer knew he was considerably less pleased now as he moved with implacable dignity to the tree. Ignoring Clarence, Dr. Hoffman merely nodded at Mr. Owl and bestowed his handshake only upon Mr. Hogarth, whom he obviously considered worthy by reason of reputation. Finally he sat down on a campstool provided by Mr. Tippet and frowningly surveyed those in front of him, like God sitting in judgment. With his great shock of white hair and white moustache and goatee, he was an impressive and commanding figure.

"This," he ground out coldly, "is the most outrageous thing I ever heard of! Where's Swimmer?"

"Right here, Doc," said Swimmer, as he limped up from the pebbly area and settled beside Clarence. "As Mr. Owl told you, I'm willing to make a deal. But first each of us will have to make a few con—con— What's the blatted word?"

"Concessions," said Clarence.

"That's right. Concessions. But Mr. Owl will explain it to you."

Dr. Hoffman seemed not to hear. He was staring at Swimmer with open-mouthed surprise. "Why," he exclaimed, "you really can talk! Somehow I couldn't quite believe it."

"Oh, he can talk," Mr. Owl said drily, "and he's not at all backward in the use of language. It should add considerably to his box-office appeal."

"Mr. Owl, I am hardly interested in box-office appeal. I am a scientist as well as a man of means."

Mr. Owl nodded, smiling faintly. "Yes, but I happen to know that your income from lecturing has gone up enormously since Swimmer began appearing with you. Therefore, before he appears again, he must have a contract giving him a percentage of the earnings."

"That is utterly ridiculous," said the doctor. "I presume you and Clarence are planning to pocket most of it?"

"Not one penny of it. There are some men, Doctor, whose minds do not happen to work that way. Clarence has an adequate pension, and I have more than I need. Our only reward will be Swimmer's friendship."

"Oh, come now," Dr. Hoffman said irritably. "What kind of game is this? Swimmer has no use for money!"

"But I have!" Swimmer burst out. "And it's a whumpdooley of a good use too! I—I want to adopt Penny Jones."

"What?"

Mr. Hogarth said, "Doctor, he has a great regard for that little redheaded girl I told you about earlier. We've explained to him about the difficulties of adoption, but Mr. Owl thinks he can work out something by which I will be the legal guardian and Swimmer a sort of contributing associate. In other words, his income would go to Penny's support and future schooling. She's a most extraordinary—"

"I have no interest whatever in extraordinary children," Dr. Hoffman interrupted coldly. "Is this the only reason you wanted a contract?"

"By no means," said Mr. Owl, smiling his odd little smile. "Swimmer insists upon several other points. First, the establishment of a summer laboratory in this section of the mountains—he prefers the trout farm, and I understand it can be bought. Next, he wants Clarence to remain with him, as usual, and he requests that Miss Primm be brought from the city, along with the white mouse and the mynah bird. Miss Primm, by the way, can be Penny's companion and governess."

After a pause, Mr. Owl went on, "We come, finally, to what could be the most important part—"

"You mean he wants *more?*" Dr. Hoffman said with thunderous sarcasm.

"Yes," Mr. Owl admitted. "And I'm sure you'll find this part uncommonly interesting. In fact, the entire world—"

"I don't want to hear it!" the doctor thundered, rising. "I've heard enough already. This is preposterous, utterly preposterous! Do you think for a moment I'd ever allow myself to be dictated to by—by an animal? An overgrown member of the weasel family? The very idea of it is revolting. When I regain possession of him—and I will— he'll be taught a lesson! Come, Tippet. Show me the way back."

Swimmer felt as if he had been slapped and kicked. He had had it all planned for Ripple to come out at this time and be introduced. Mr. Owl and Mr. Hogarth had already met her, and they had really flipped. Mr. Owl had said, "Why, she's just as you described her, Swimmer. She's as cute as a water bug and as bright as a chickadee!" And Mr. Hogarth had added, "What a pair you'll make! Dr. Hoffman's bound to love her."

But now the bright vision of Ripple and himself wearing silver bells onstage together went glimmering.

Swimmer stared, stricken, at the doctor's retreating back. "You—you—" he burst out. Then he found his tongue and cried, "Sure, maybe I am an overgrown weasel. But I'd rather be that than a puffed-up member of the ape family, like you! That's what you are—a skrinky old swelled-up blattheaded ape!"

Dr. Hoffman paused briefly and glared backward, mouth agape as if he could not believe his ears. Mr. Hogarth chuckled and said, "You tell 'im, Swimmer—and I'll tell the world!"

For a while afterward silence held them.

Presently Mr. Hogarth said, "I'd like to talk to Penny again, if I can find her."

"If you can locate her," said Mr. Owl, "I'd like to meet her."

Clarence said, "I'd better go along with you. I want to see her myself, and there are some points of law you can straighten me out on."

Long after they had gone, Swimmer sat glumly under the tree, watching Ripple and Willow fish in the pool, while he waited for Clarence to return. He would have joined them just to take his mind off things, only, for no reason at all it seemed, his leg had begun to hurt worse than ever. But maybe it was just the rotty situation. He had never felt so low.

Suddenly his attention was attracted by happy chirruping in the upper part of the pool. Now, instead of two dark heads in the water, there were four. The other two seemed to be a pair of much older otters who were Willow's friends.

He had no heart for meeting them, but he watched them curiously until Ripple came back, bringing him a fish. She touched her cold nose to his and settled on the grass beside him.

In answer to his question, she explained that the visitors were her mother's mother and father. She added, *They want us to go down to the river with them.*

Is Willow going? he asked.

Yes.

And you?

I will go where you go, she told him. *For as long as we have life. We can be happy without silver bells.*

A great warmth filled his heart. *You are right. But it would have been great to wear the bells together, and answer people's questions and make fun of their crazy ways. And I wanted you to see the world.*

This is our world, she reminded him.

I wanted us to have a little of both worlds, he explained. *That way we would always have Penny and Clarence for friends. But now, when this is over, we may never see them again.*

It is far from over, came her thought, and he could feel the uneasiness in her.

Swimmer also had been vaguely uneasy ever since Clarence left, and now the feeling began to grow. He wondered if Snake Eyes had anything to do with it. Had the trapper really gone away, or was he hiding somewhere, waiting until there was no one around to see what he did? The very thought of Snake Eyes could always bring a chill creeping through him.

His mind turned to Penny, and he felt a little sick. Now that he couldn't help her, what was going to become of her?

He was not surprised when Willow, at last, came up and briefly touched noses with Ripple and himself. When she re-entered the creek and slipped downstream it was with the understanding that she would see them again on her regular rounds during the weeks ahead.

With her mother gone, Ripple crept closer to Swimmer for comfort, and they waited while the shadows lengthened and deepened. It seemed that Clarence would never return.

It was long after dark when Clarence finally got back. Swimmer knew instantly that he was deeply concerned about something.

98

"Did you find Penny?" he said, almost afraid to ask questions.

"No," Clarence mumbled. "She must have got hungry and gone back to the trout farm. I sure wish we'd located her first. Mr. Owl was ready to take her home with him until Mr. Hogarth could get a decent family to look after her."

Swimmer waited. There was something else in the back of Clarence's mind, and it had to do with Snake Eyes. But Clarence began talking about the trout farm instead.

"That's a mighty pretty little place, Swimmer," he said, as he broke up twigs to start a small fire. "First time I saw it I thought how I'd like to own it and retire there. Doesn't look like that'll happen now, but, at least, I bought up the mortgage on it."

"You—you bought the trout farm mortgage from the bank?" Swimmer exclaimed.

"Well, I had Mr. Owl do it for me this morning, so folks wouldn't know. You see, by my buying the mortgage, we figured we'd get Mr. Sykes to sell the place if we offered a good price. When I found out he still had his old farm he could move back to, I offered better than a good price if he'd sell and move out immediately."

Clarence sighed and shook his head. "It didn't work. Not even with an overdue mortgage hanging over him that could be foreclosed. He sure is a no-account stubborn buzzard!"

Swimmer had only a hazy idea of such matters. "Couldn't you foreclose and drive the scumpy weasel off?" he asked hopefully.

"No," said Clarence. "It takes forever to pry a man loose from his property that way. There are scads of laws to protect him. I thought sure I could get old Doc to handle it—with all his money he'd manage to get it right away if he

99

wanted it. But that didn't work, either. Now, I don't know what to do."

"Why don't you tell me about Snake Eyes?" Swimmer said uneasily.

Clarence looked at him sharply. He sighed again. "Reckon I'd better. You've got to know the worst. I think that rascal wants to kill you."

"No!"

"I'm afraid he does, old pal."

"But why? What makes you so sure?"

"It's like this," said Clarence. "When I left Mr. Owl and Mr. Hogarth at the road I figured I'd better do a little scouting, just for safety's sake. When we were looking for Penny we found where Snake Eyes and his man have their truck hidden, so we knew Doc had probably hired 'em to stick around until he could get that restraining order changed—which he'll do, sure as anything.

"Anyway, when I found where those trappers were camped, I had one of those funny feelings like I get sometimes. So I slipped back there and did some listening. That devilish black dog made it hard—I had to keep downwind and stay in the smoke of their campfire, so he wouldn't sniff me. And I didn't dare get too close, either. So I could only catch a word now and then. But I caught enough. Snake Eyes hates you. And he's scared of you."

"Hates me? Scared of me? But why?"

"Because you can talk," said Clarence. "He's superstitious, and it really shook him. He hates you for the things you said to him—and he's scared of you for the things you haven't said. He's got the idea you can read his mind."

"Pshaw, his own dog can do that."

"But he doesn't know it. All he knows is that he's done things he wouldn't want the world to hear about. Jake would like to catch you and hold you for ransom, and put

100

the squeeze on Doc, for Doc would pay big. But Jake's afraid to try it. He's superstitious too. So they both decided they'd better get rid of you, and fast."

Swimmer was shocked. "Aw, fiffle," he muttered, glancing at Ripple. "Now, we'll have to find another den. Maybe we'd better—"

He stopped, for Ripple was suddenly alert. Then he caught the dog scent on the night breeze. It was Scruff's scent, and now he could hear the big dog coming swiftly down through the woods, making no effort to conceal his movements. Something must be very wrong for Scruff to act that way.

Seconds later the tawny beast reached the edge of the firelight. He halted abruptly and gave a low urgent growl.

Clarence, startled, leaped to his feet. But Swimmer said, "It's about Penny. Something's happened. He wants me to come and help."

9

He Releases a Prisoner

*C*larence said quickly, "Try to find out where she is, and what's wrong."

Swimmer looked at Scruff a moment and reported, "She's locked up somewhere. A sort of small place, and not far from the house. He'll lead me to it. He thinks I can handle the lock."

"Maybe you can, but you've no business going up there alone."

"Aw, don't treat me like a gloop. Scruff will be with me, and he can sure lick anything I can't."

"Wait," said Clarence. "There are too many things coming to a head at once. Let me think a minute." He stood scowling into the dark while he rubbed his long jaw. Abruptly he said, "We'll all go, at least as far as the fence. And, Swimmer, I'd better carry you."

"Huh? What for?"

"Now who's acting like a gloop? When we leave here, we're not coming back. Do you want that devilish hound to trail you to the next place? He knows your scent."

Swiftly Clarence trod out the tiny fire and soaked the embers with a cup of water. He threw his sleeping bag and knapsack over one shoulder and lifted Swimmer to the other. Finally he reached for his hiking stick and hesitated. "Where's Willow?"

"Gone traveling with friends. She won't be back."

"Good! If Snake Eyes comes, he'll gas an empty tree. Let's go."

There was only starlight overhead, and not much of it sifted down through the trees, but Swimmer had little trouble keeping Scruff in sight. Clarence, though, was forced to use his flashlight continually, and he moved slowly up the long slope, taking care not to stumble. Ripple was a silent shadow, gliding between the dog and the man.

They crossed the winding brook that splashed down from the trout pools and at last gained the fence. It was an old barbed-wire affair overgrown with honeysuckle. While Scruff waited impatiently on the other side, Clarence set Swimmer down with a grunt of relief and peered through the dim apple orchard beyond.

"You used to weigh twenty-seven pounds," he muttered under his breath, "but now it feels like a hundred. H'mm. I've got really good night vision, but I can't make out any buildings from here."

"I can," said Swimmer. "Why don't I go ahead with Scruff? If I can't open the place she's locked in, I'll come back for you."

"Okay. But watch it, pal. If you have any trouble with that dog up there, let Scruff handle him. Tell Scruff to chase him 'way off to one side to divert attention."

Swimmer crept under the fence. Ripple followed.

You had better stay here, he told her. *There may be trouble.*

Then you will need me. We must learn to work together.

Silently they followed Scruff through the orchard. Swimmer limped confidently, his bad leg forgotten as his senses sharpened to the many messages brought on the night breeze. They rounded the lower trout pond, crept past the side of a small barn Swimmer had seen from the fence, then all three stopped abruptly.

Directly ahead, shrouded by evergreens, lay the trout farm cottage. From one lower window came a dull glow of light. Off to the left, and much too close to the cottage for comfort, were three small buildings. Swimmer realized instantly that Penny must be in one of them, even though he had not yet caught her scent. But Tattle's scent was strong from the area to the right of the lighted window.

Swimmer had barely scented and located Tattle, when the fickle breeze turned and began to come from the opposite direction. It was the worst thing that could have happened.

Swiftly, for the three of them were aware of the danger on the instant, they headed for the group of small buildings. But they had covered less than half the distance when Tattle caught the scent of the invaders and set up a wild and almost hysterical yapping.

Get him! Swimmer ordered Scruff. *We'll find Penny.*

As Scruff charged, he and Ripple raced for the nearest building. From the direction of the cottage came a sudden snarl followed by a frightened shriek from Tattle.

Precious seconds were lost before Swimmer discovered that Penny was not in the first building but in the third. As he reached up to find out how the latch worked, he could hear her dry sobs inside. He started to call out to her, but thought better of it. Someone else might hear him. And what if he couldn't open the door?

It didn't have a regular lock, but a hasp that folded over a staple. Thrust down through the staple, securing it against all possibility of being opened from within, was an old screwdriver.

Ordinarily such a simple arrangement would have given him no trouble at all. But the screwdriver had been rammed down through the staple with such force that he was unable to budge it. Nor could he reach high enough to grasp it by the handle and pull it upward. It had to be pushed from below, and he could stand on only one foot to do it.

Somewhere in the distance Swimmer could hear Tattle's panicky yelps as he dodged for his life. Over in the cottage lights suddenly came on, flooding the porch and the pools. A door slammed. Someone cursed and ran outside, and a spotlight swept the barn and the orchard. Seconds later there was the sharp report of a rifle.

As he struggled frantically with the screwdriver, he heard another shot and then another. He knew it was Weaver's rifle, for it had the same sound as the weapon that had been used against him days ago. Desperately he tugged and twisted, but the jammed metal held tight.

Suddenly another small pair of "hands" like his own was helping, and Ripple was adding her strength to the upward thrust. All at once the screwdriver loosened, and seconds later they were inside.

"It's us!" he gulped to the huddled form on the floor, his gnome voice sounding very froglike in his haste. "Scruff brought us the word. Quick—let's get out of here!"

"But—but—I don't know what to do," Penny sobbed. "I —I—I've no place to go."

"Yes, you have—you've got friends, now. Hurry!"

As she got uncertainly to her feet, Swimmer plucked at the scrap of tarpaulin she was clutching tightly about her and drew her outside. He realized at once that her eyes were so swollen now that she could hardly see.

"Lead her, Ripple," he said aloud. "This way."

Ripple caught a corner of the tarpaulin between her teeth, and they started around the corner of the building in a direction that would take them well away from the trout pools and the barn. They had barely reached the orchard when there was another shot. Before the echo of it had died away, they were startled by a piercing cry of pain and fright.

"Pa!" Weaver Sykes yelled shrilly. "Pa! Help me, Pa! I'm caught!"

Penny gasped. "Oh, dear! I knew it would happen! I just knew it."

"Knew what?" Swimmer muttered, not in the least concerned over Weaver's agonies. His worry was for Scruff. From the moment the big dog had started the diversion, Swimmer had been aware of Scruff out there, drawing the attention away from them. But at the sound of the last shot the connection had been broken. It had been broken by a bullet.

"It's that awful last trap," Penny was saying. "The one Mr. Sykes refused to look for. It was the biggest of all—and now Weaver's caught in it!"

"Let 'im stay caught," Swimmer growled. "He—he shot Scruff."

"Oh, no!" Penny wailed. "Scruff's my friend! Where is he? Help me find him!"

"Clarence will take care of him if he's still alive. It happened down there near the fence where Clarence is waiting. Let's get moving!"

To Weaver's cries were now added more sounds from the cottage. A door banged, there were angry oaths, and someone pounded across a porch, down the steps, and out upon the gravel. Once, through the trees, Swimmer glimpsed the hurrying form of Grady Sykes vaguely outlined by the cottage lights.

Penny could not move fast, and it seemed to take forever to reach the fence across the lower slope of the orchard.

They had come out, Swimmer figured, a good hundred yards or more from the spot where he had left Clarence.

When they had crawled under the wire, he said to Penny, "If you'll wait here with Ripple, I'll go and get Clarence. We'll be heading in this direction anyway."

"Aw'right," Penny whispered. "And—and please excuse me for being a crybaby. But when you get tired of trying to tough it out, it sort of helps."

"Aw, fiffle, everybody has to cry," Swimmer told her. "Even otters."

If you haven't cried, you haven't lived, he thought, as he began following the fence toward Clarence. He had cried more than once in his life, and the way he felt at the moment he was on the edge of doing it again. He wouldn't have believed he could feel this way over a ding-blatted old dog, practically his born enemy. But Scruff was different.

When he reached the right place along the fence, the only sign of Clarence was his scent. Of Clarence himself he could see nothing. But he could hear voices. At last he made out two dark shapes far over on the right where the brook from the trout pools curved down under the fence.

"But I can't stand up, Pa," Weaver Sykes whined. "It hurts something awful. I think my leg's broke."

"Your dang leg ain't broke! You oughta had better sense than to step down in that water, slap in the one place I told you to keep away from. Of all the tomfool—"

"But I couldn't help it, Pa! I'd just shot that big varmint of a dog. I seen 'im fall, an' I was running to git close enough to finish 'im off—"

"You sure you seen 'im fall?"

"Sure I seen 'im! I ain't blind."

"Then where is he now?"

"Danged if I know! If he's gunshot . . ."

"He'll be meaner'n a bear. We'd better git back to the

107

house. C'mon, Weaver, I done freed your foot but I don't aim to carry you. Git up an' try to walk."

Swimmer had heard enough to piece together what had happened. Suddenly he turned and crept carefully over to the curving bank of the brook and followed it a few yards downstream. Almost immediately he found Clarence crouched under the edge of the bank holding Scruff's limp body.

"Is—is he dead?" Swimmer gulped.

"No. His heart's still beating. Where's Penny?"

Swimmer explained, and he added, "Her eyes are swollen shut."

"Oh, lordy!" Clarence shook his head. "This calls for some tall thinking. Those Sykes fellows gone yet?"

"They've just left."

"Well, we can't stay here, so I reckon I'll carry Scruff over to where Penny is. We'll figure it out from there."

Swimmer wondered how Clarence was going to manage such a load, for he was still carrying the sleeping bag and knapsack. But the black man merely crouched, pulled Scruff's body over his left shoulder with one hand, and thrust himself upright with his hiking stick.

A few minutes later they reached the spot where Penny and Ripple were waiting, and the big dog was gently lowered to the ground. Penny held back her tears while Clarence carefully examined Scruff with the aid of his flashlight.

"It's a head wound," Clarence muttered finally. "Doesn't look too bad, but it grazed the skull. Knocked him out cold. Good thing I was close enough to see him fall, and that Weaver stepped in the trap. Otherwise he'd be a dead dog now."

"But—but how long before he'll wake up?" Penny asked tremulously.

108

Clarence sighed wearily. "It's a concussion, so it might take hours. And he'll probably be shaky for sometime afterward."

"W-what are we going to do?"

"That's just what I'm trying to figure," he said slowly. "Penny, how far is the nearest telephone from here?"

"Oh, goodness, it must be miles and miles. Mr. Sykes has the only one between the gap and the bridge."

"H'mm. Before I could walk to a phone, it would probably be after midnight, and I'm the wrong color to be knocking on somebody's door at that hour. Now, let me think . . ."

"Who did you want to phone?" Swimmer asked.

"Mr. Hogarth. Thought I might get him to come out and take Penny some place for the night."

Swimmer said, "Why not call Mr. Owl?"

"He's not home. If we had found Penny earlier, he'd planned to take her back to his place and skip a meeting he was going to in Asheville. But he went on to the meeting, and I understand he was going to spend the night with friends. So . . ."

Clarence spread his hands and looked worriedly at Penny. She was huddled under her scrap of tarpaulin, shivering in the mountain chill. It was turning colder.

"Penny," he said, "we've got to camp somewhere tonight, but we can't do it here, and we'll have to stay away from the creek. Do you know of a spot to the west of us where there's a spring?"

"Oh, s-s-sure," she said, trying to keep her teeth from chattering. "If—if you'll j-just k-keep walking straight ahead p-past the corner of the fence, you'll come to a n-nice spring that runs down through the rocks. Clarence, h-have you any ch-ch-chocolate left?"

"Chocolate? Say, I'll bet those rascals didn't give you any

supper, and I know you didn't have any lunch. Lordy me! Two chocolate bars coming up, and there'll be tea and tuna fish as soon as we make camp."

Clarence fumbled in his knapsack, produced the chocolate, and said, "We'll wait while you eat one bar now, then we'd better move on and find our camp. Swimmer, you lead the way, and I'll follow behind Penny. Er, Penny, can you see by holding one eye open with your fingers?"

She tried it while she munched chocolate. "Oh, I can see just fine by doing that. Well, good enough, anyway."

When they were ready to go, Clarence gave Penny his flashlight and followed close behind her, holding Scruff on his shoulder with one arm, and using his stick to brace himself as he moved along. Swimmer wound in and out between the crowding trees and ledges of rock, trying to pick the easiest path. Every few yards he stopped and waited while Ripple, with a corner of the tarpaulin in her mouth, guided Penny's feet around protruding roots that might have tripped her.

The main sound of the night was the steady roar of the creek far down on the left. But presently Swimmer could make out a new sound of water, a soft splashing this was, directly ahead. Yet with their slow progress it was long minutes before they reached the thicket of evergreens hiding the tiny stream.

Clarence placed Scruff on the ground and briefly explored the thicket. Finally he moved Scruff inside to an open spot under a ledge, gathered twigs and dry hemlock needles, and soon had a fire going.

"Nice place," he said approvingly, as he unrolled his sleeping bag. "Out of sight and out of the wind. Okay, Penny, give me your tarp, and hop in the bag."

"B-b-but I can't take your sleeping bag!" she protested.

110

"Besides, I'm not a bit c-c-cold. Well, not very m-m-much, anyway."

"Aw, fiffle," said Swimmer. "Do as he tells you before he bops you."

She giggled, drew off the piece of tarpaulin, and slid quickly into the bag.

Clarence set a small pan of water to heat on the fire, then took several cans of tuna fish from his knapsack. Opening one, he gave it to Penny along with a fork and a paper napkin.

"Eat it slowly," he ordered, "and save the napkin. We'll need it to help clean things afterward." He looked at Swimmer and Ripple. "How about you two? Are you hungry?"

"We had trout earlier," Swimmer said. "And there are crawfish here if we want 'em."

"That's good," said Clarence. "We've only a few cans left. We'll save one for Scruff, and divvy up the rest for breakfast."

It suddenly came to Swimmer that though Clarence himself hadn't eaten since morning, he was going to make do with a chocolate bar and save the fish for Penny and the others. As he watched Clarence bathe Penny's eyes, using a cloth moistened with some of the water he was boiling for tea, he realized how deeply concerned the man was about all of them. At the bottom of his worry was the broken-down van.

"Clarence," he asked presently, "are you planning to hike to town in the morning?"

"I'm figuring on it. It's a three-hour hike, and I want to be there by the time things open. If the van isn't fixed, I'll rent a car—or buy an old one if I have to. I couldn't do it Sunday, and there wasn't time to do it today. You see, old pal, we've got to have transportation. Without it . . ."

Clarence paused. Penny, who had been propped against him while he bathed her swollen face, had fallen asleep. In her exhaustion she had not even finished her can of fish. Clarence made her comfortable for the night in the sleeping bag and shook his head.

"Poor kid," he muttered. "She's had all she can take." He turned and studied Scruff, who had not yet moved, then stretched out by the fire on Penny's scrap of tarpaulin.

"I don't like it, Swimmer," Clarence confided. "If Scruff were okay, I wouldn't worry. But somehow I hate to go off and leave all of you here."

"Aw, nobody's going to find us," Swimmer told him, trying to sound more convincing than he felt.

"Oh, I'm sure they won't, but it's just how I feel. I keep feeling I ought to wait till Penny's had a good rest, then all of us should start out for Mr. Owl's place. But that doesn't make sense. I haven't the least idea where Mr. Owl lives, except that it's over the gap somewhere. It could be twenty miles from here.

"Besides," Clarence went on, "he's not due back till late tomorrow. His daughter keeps house for him, but I understand she's away too. So that's out. Town's the best bet. Penny might be in no shape to walk tomorrow, or Scruff either. What we need is a car."

"You could be right," Swimmer admitted. "But somehow I make out better with feelings than with thoughts."

Ripple chose this moment of uncertainty in Clarence to go over and clasp his long black hand between her small webbed ones.

"Cla-wence," she said, almost as if she were a small bright child. She tried to go on, but the words would not come.

"Hey!" Clarence whispered in delight. "How'd you learn to say my name?"

112

"She catches on fast," Swimmer said proudly. "I told you she was bright as a chickadee. She's trying to tell you not to decide on anything tonight. You're always wiser in the morning."

"I hope she's right," Clarence told him. He frowned at the mist creeping about them, then built up the fire and stretched out again to sleep.

But no one slept soundly that night save Penny and Scruff. Both were still dead to the world when Clarence got up hours later, piled more wood on the fire, and put on water for tea. The mist was almost solid about them now, and Clarence said little until he was ready to go.

At that moment Scruff lifted his head and tried to rise.

"Easy," said Clarence, patting him happily, then he opened one of the cans of tuna he had been saving. "Here's your breakfast, old boy. Help Swimmer and Ripple hold down the fort, and I'll be back as soon as possible."

It wasn't until the black man had vanished in the mist, and his footsteps could no longer be heard, that Swimmer became aware of an unpleasant truth: Clarence had made the wrong decision.

10

He Makes a Deal

Swimmer did not question the way he felt. It came from a sudden sense of danger that he could not have explained. Though it had neither sound nor scent, the danger was out there, surely, and he knew that Clarence should have waited until daylight. As soon as they could see through the mist, it would be much better if they all tried to find Mr. Owl's place.

Uneasily he waited while the darkness grayed. The mist did not worry him. Instead, he hoped it would thicken and remain through the morning, for it might be a protection.

It was almost daylight when Penny stirred. Abruptly she sat up in the sleeping bag, a frightened look on her face. Instantly Scruff moved over beside her and thrust his cold nose against her cheek. The frightened look vanished.

"Oh, Scruff!" she cried and threw her arms around him. "I—I didn't know where I was for a moment. Golly, I'm so glad you're all right!"

"He's not quite all right, yet," Swimmer said. "He tells me he's got a whumper of a headache, and he's kind of wobbly besides. I told him what happened, and he says he's sorry he didn't finish off Tattle, but he'd just got his teeth into the scump when the lights went out."

"That poor silly Tattle," she said. "He was just trying to do his duty."

"Duty my eye!" Swimmer grumbled. "He's a scumpy weasel, and I wish I'd drowned 'im when I had the chance." He paused and studied her earnestly. "How—how do you feel this morning?"

"Oh, I'm just fine."

Judging by her looks, Swimmer didn't think fine was the right word. "But your eyes," he went on. "Can you see all right?"

"I—I think so. But I can tell better after I wash my face at the spring. Where's the flashlight?"

Swimmer almost groaned. If her eyes were any better, she wouldn't need the flashlight now.

"Clarence took it, so he could find his way to the road," he explained. "He's hiking to town to get the van if it's fixed, or maybe a car, or something."

"Oh." Penny was silent a moment. At last she said uneasily, "I—I hope he gets back soon."

Swimmer knew Clarence couldn't possibly return for hours and hours—unless, of course, he was lucky enough to find Mr. Hogarth right away and get his help. But Swimmer had an unpleasant feeling that Mr. Hogarth was also away somewhere, like Mr. Owl, and that this wasn't going to be the most pleasant of days for any of them.

He watched Ripple go up to Penny and take her hand. "Pen-ny," she managed to say slowly. "I . . . help . . ."

Penny gave a little cry of delight and hugged Ripple. "I knew you could talk if you tried!"

Swimmer said, "She's trying to tell you she'll take you to the spring, and—and lead you when we leave . . ."

"L-leave?" Penny faltered. "You think we'd better leave here?"

"I sure do. Just as soon as we can."

115

Even as he spoke he could hear the distant cough and mutter of the trapper's hound. It was so very faint he doubted that Penny was aware of it, but he knew Ripple was, as well as Scruff. In the heavy mist the sound might have been difficult to locate, but he did not have to guess that it came from the area of the beech tree. This was the hour when Snake Eyes would slip down there unseen to gas the den.

While Penny hurriedly bathed her eyes at the spring, Swimmer wondered what Snake Eyes would do when he found the den empty. Of course, he'd depend on the hound to find a trail. And when there wasn't any trail . . .

Suddenly Swimmer went cold. He hadn't left a trail that the black dog could follow, but he'd forgotten what a mountain mist could do. It could blot everything from sight and hide you—but as it crept past, damp and clinging, it could pick up your scent and carry it along for a great distance.

The mist was drifting in the general direction of the beech, and it wouldn't be long before the hound became aware of his scent. No matter how faint and uncertain it was at first, the hound would surely recognize it and try to follow it to its source.

Swimmer fretted over this and waited impatiently while Penny returned from the spring. With Ripple's help, she located the remaining cans of fish and began struggling with the can opener. It gave him a sinking sensation to realize that her eyes were no better than they had been last night. To see at all she was forced to hold her eyelids apart with her fingers as Clarence had told her to do.

Somehow she got the cans open and the contents divided between the four of them. They had barely started to eat when Swimmer heard the hound again. It seemed closer this time.

116

Penny bit her lip. "Was—was that a dog I heard?"

"Yes," Swimmer muttered unhappily. "It was that dirty trapper's hound. Hurry and eat!"

"Oh, dear! Mr. Sykes is just mean, but that man frightens me. There's something awful about him. Do—do you think he'll come up here?"

"He sure will if his dog gets my scent. He hates my gizzard. Penny, do you know where Mr. Owl lives?"

"I—I've never been to his place, but I think it's the first farm over the gap."

"Then let's go there. We'd better start now before it's too late. Ripple will lead you to the road."

"Wait," said Penny. "If Clarence comes and finds we've gone—" She stood gnawing on her lower lip a moment, then suddenly stooped and fumbled through the ashes of the fire. Swimmer saw her pick up a charred stick. Carefully holding one eye open, she used the stick to draw the outline of an owl upon a flat rock beside the sleeping bag.

"That ought to do it," she said and clutched the scrap of tarpaulin about her as Ripple started to lead her away. "But let's not go to the road," she added. "Mr. Sykes may be looking for me there. I—I once saw an old trail up here somewhere that the lumbermen used. It'll take us to the gap."

Scruff knew about the trail and soon found it for them. It was overgrown and little traveled save by deer, but the going was much easier on it. Now Penny was able to move without stumbling and falling.

With every forward step Swimmer felt better. They were beginning to climb now, and he knew the gap couldn't be too far away. If they could reach it and cross it, even if they had to go the rest of the way on the road . . .

But his hopes went tumbling as he heard, somewhere in the mist behind them, a single short low bark from the hound. It was nowhere near the creek, and it told him as plainly as words could that his scent had been discovered. He could almost hear Snake Eyes saying, "Go find 'im, Devil!"

He knew Penny heard the dog too, for she paused a moment to listen, then spoke urgently to Ripple and plunged on, trying to move faster. But it was lost effort. She had taken only a few steps when she stumbled and fell. Scruff, who had been leading the way, stopped and stood swaying as if it were all he could do to stay on his feet.

In his sudden despair Swimmer's leg, which never seemed to bother him when things were going right, began to throb miserably. They are bound to catch up with us soon, he thought. What are we going to do?

The answer came. He must fight the black hound while the others went on. There was no other way.

Swimmer had no sooner made his decision when he realized that Scruff had picked up his thought. *You are crippled,* Scruff told him. *The black dog is too big for you to kill. But I can do it easily.*

You have been hurt, Swimmer said. *You are not able to fight.*

It will not be a fight, Scruff reminded him. *My legs are uncertain, but my jaws are strong. Bring him close to my jaws, and I will kill in an instant.*

And to Swimmer's mind came a picture of the way Scruff killed. It was not by the throat, as he had supposed, but with a single savage snap that broke the victim's neck. Only a creature as large and powerful as Scruff would be capable of such a feat.

Even so, Swimmer had his misgivings. But it seemed like a good plan, and there was no time to think of another one. As he searched the trail ahead, looking for a place to carry out the plan, he heard the hound again. It was very close now, and he knew Snake Eyes couldn't be far behind it, if he wasn't actually holding the leash.

That log yonder, he said urgently to Scruff. *Hide at the end of it, and I will bring the black dog to you.*

Scruff almost fell behind the great rotting log that edged the trail. Beyond him, entirely unaware of what was happening, Penny was being tugged away by a knowing Ripple. Already they were fading into the mist.

The trap was set. But as Swimmer limped back a few yards to be ready to meet the hound, the swirling mist about him cleared momentarily and the morning sun cut through. Far behind, where the trail dipped down the misty slope, he glimpsed the hound, straining at his leash, coming into view. He could just make out the vague head and shoulders of the man behind it. The man was Snake Eyes, and he seemed to be carrying a club in one hand.

As Swimmer turned, the hound sighted him. It leaped forward with a sudden roar, jerking the leash free. Snake Eyes cursed and lunged after the dog, crying hoarsely, "Kill 'im, Devil! Kill the varmint!"

Devil charged with such speed that Swimmer, who had started back slowly, barely made it to the log. As he sped around the end of it, with the snarling beast almost upon him, Scruff leaped for Devil's neck. But Scruff's wobbly legs were far too slow. He missed the hound entirely, and abruptly Swimmer found himself fighting for his life.

The black hound was fast, powerful, and vicious, and four times Swimmer's weight. Swimmer felt the hot breath and the slash of teeth across his flank and whirled away, turning and snapping. Only his natural quickness saved him from a bloody mauling. As the sun vanished and the mist closed about them again, he darted in and managed to seize one of his enemy's hind legs. Clinging to it grimly and praying for Scruff to make his move, he became aware of

Snake Eyes hurrying up the trail, cursing and yelling for Jake and the rifle.

Why didn't Scruff come? In a few more seconds it would be too late.

All at once the black dog was knocked from its feet. Its snarling stopped as Scruff's great jaws clamped upon its neck. Swimmer loosened his hold on the instant and spun about to face Snake Eyes, who was rushing upon him with upraised stick.

At this moment, as Swimmer came face-to-face with his ancient and deadly enemy, all his fear and mounting fury turned into an overpowering force within him that exploded into a scream. It was the terrible cry of his kind that is given only in an extremity. No sound made by a human is even half as piercing or as paralyzing, for it can be heard more than a mile. As Swimmer screamed, he charged with hackles raised, and the stick that might have brained him dropped from nerveless hands. At the same time something unseen streaked from the brush behind Snake Eyes and bit him furiously in the leg.

It hardly needed the extra horror of a killer dog with frightful jaws to break the trapper's nerve. The scream and Ripple's bite had already done that. Snake Eyes gave a strangled cry and fled.

Swimmer found a frightened Penny crouched behind the tree where Ripple had left her.

"Whew!" she breathed in relief, after everything had been explained to her. "I—I thought all the banshees everywhere had suddenly cut loose! And that awful hound; I didn't know a dog could make me so scared. But I can't help feeling sorry for him now, the poor thing."

"Aw, fiffle," Swimmer muttered, and added philosophically, "We come and we go. It was his time to go, the rotty scump, and I say good riddance. Now let's find Mr. Owl's place."

They reached the gap a quarter of an hour later, and came out into bright sunlight. The road was only a few yards away on their right. It wound down, Swimmer saw, past a small, white farmhouse in the little valley below. But the trail also led to the farm, only it went through the woods behind the house.

There was traffic on the road, and Swimmer didn't know what people would think of a runaway girl with two black eyes, in the company of a wild dog with the staggers. Considering that she was being very carefully led by a pair of talking otters, he decided they had better keep to the trail. He just hoped the white farmhouse was Mr. Owl's place.

They reached the farm woods late that morning. After crossing a footbridge over a spring, they wound past a duck pond full of staring ducks and started for the house. Near the kitchen, two brown spaniels appeared suddenly and dashed toward them, barking furiously. Scruff, though he seemed hardly able to stand by now, spoke to them only once, and immediately they knuckled under and became quite friendly.

It was soon evident that no one was at home. Swimmer was still wondering whether this was the right farm when a small truck rolled into the yard, stopped, and a pleasant-faced Indian woman got out carrying a bag of groceries.

He limped over to her and asked hopefully, "Are—are you Miss Owl, ma'am?"

She gasped, nearly dropped the bag, and exclaimed, "Why—why, you must be Swimmer! Father's told me about you. Yes, I'm Mary Owl. What in the world—" She stared at Penny. "You have to be Penny Jones! What have those awful people done to you? You poor child—come right in the house!"

Things happened fast after that.

Penny, though she protested that she was "feeling just fine—well, not too awful, anyway," was put to bed immediately and a doctor summoned. Before the doctor could get there, a very worried Clarence and a grim Mr. Hogarth arrived in Mr. Hogarth's car. They had gone to the empty camp, found Penny's owl drawing, and rushed to the farm. Mr. Hogarth was busy taking pictures of Penny's bruises when Mr. Owl returned. After seeing Penny, Mr. Owl went into an immediate huddle with Clarence and Mr. Hogarth. In the middle of this the doctor came.

The doctor turned out to be a blood brother of Mr. Owl. He bandaged Penny's eyes with a Cherokee poultice and made her promise to stay in bed for at least three days under threat of losing her scalp. Afterward he carefully examined Swimmer's leg, then went out to check on Scruff, who had retreated to the barn. It took a word from Clarence before Scruff would let the doctor near him, but after that it was all right.

Miss Owl fixed up a comfortable corner of the barn for Scruff to recuperate in and gave him all the food he could eat. Then she turned the duck pond over to Swimmer and Ripple.

"It's full of sunfish," she said, "and you can have all of them you want. Just don't give the ducks a bad time."

And Clarence added, "Whatever you do, don't stray off the farm, or even go too far from the pond. Until Mr. Owl can get some things straightened out, he doesn't want anyone to know you're here."

After all he had been through, Swimmer wasn't about to leave the farm. As for the pond, it was pure heaven in the beginning. He couldn't help giving the ducks a bad time at first, because it was such fun to play tag with Ripple around the flock, then suddenly pop up in the middle of them, chattering and barking. It almost drove the poor things out of their ever-loving minds. But this grew tame in a day or two. By now Clarence had the van back, and it soon became evident that something was going on.

Penny was aware of it too, and on the fourth morning—her first day outside—she hurried down to the pond to find out what Swimmer knew. Her bruises still showed, but the swelling was gone from her eyes, and Swimmer thought she was looking really special in the new clothes Miss Owl had given her.

"But what's Clarence doing?" she said. "Haven't you any idea?"

"How could I? I haven't even seen him since he got the van back. Why don't you ask him?"

"But I did ask him. And you know what he told me? He said, 'Penny, just keep your fingers crossed, and do a lot of praying.' Well, I've been praying, but I don't know what for."

"Well, keep it up," Swimmer advised. "If Clarence told you that, it's bound to be important."

Just how important it was, they had to wait a full week to learn. Early one afternoon Penny, closely followed by Scruff, dashed down to the pond and called them. "Hurry!" she cried. "Clarence wants to take us all for a ride."

As Swimmer crawled into the van he saw that the big keyboard-and-tabs machine had been removed, as well as his old cage. Now it contained only Clarence's sleeping bag and camping equipment. It surprised him when Scruff scrambled in behind Ripple without any urging. "Boy, how you've changed!" he said to the big dog. "A week ago you wouldn't have gone near a car. What's Clarence done to you?"

"Pshaw," said Clarence. "He knows he's one of the family now. And he's got a job ahead of him."

"A job?" said Swimmer, uncomprehending. Suddenly he saw what was in Clarence's mind, and he realized the black man was very uneasy about what might happen that afternoon. "Ump!" Swimmer exclaimed. "Why didn't you let me know—"

"Are you reading my mind?" Clarence interrupted.

"I sure am—the whole thing!"

"Then keep your big mouth shut, cross your webbed 'fingers,' and pray. Because it may not work."

Penny, who had started to ask a question, pressed a hand over her lips and held up crossed fingers. She managed to keep silent while the van climbed through the gap and curved down into the forested area. But when Clarence turned into the trout farm entrance, Penny gasped in dismay.

"Wha—wha—what are you going in *here* for?"

"Because it's ours," Clarence said quietly.

"Ours?"

"Yep. Yours and mine and Swimmer's and Ripple's and Scruff's. Scruff's job is the guard department. He's to keep away trappers, bears—I've always been scared of bears—and hunters, poachers, skrinks, blattheads, and all kinds of scumpy weasels."

Penny giggled. "But—but—how—"

"How'd I get rid of the weasel that was here? Easy. Mr. Owl just showed him some of those pictures Mr. Hogarth took of you, and told him he'd have to be out of here in five days or he'd go to jail for child-beating. I didn't even offer a good price this time—figured he didn't deserve it. He went back to that old farm of his, and I'm mighty glad it's in another county."

"Oh, golly, I just can't believe it!" Penny whispered. "But —but what about Welfare? What if they won't let me stay?"

"Pshaw, they haven't anything to say about it now. Mr.

Owl's fixed it up so Mr. Hogarth is in charge of you. Swimmer's in the deal too, so you could almost say he's adopted you!"

Penny was speechless for a moment. Suddenly she turned and hugged Swimmer.

"But you've got to keep on praying," Clarence added uneasily. "There's a lot to be settled yet, and you can't move in till it is."

"But—but what—"

"You'll see in a little while."

Clarence swung into the parking area near the house. Two cars were already there, and as Swimmer followed the others out of the van he saw Mr. Hogarth talking to Mr. Owl by the upper trout pool. Near them was a new card table with some papers on it, and several new chairs that Clarence must have bought.

As he visioned what was coming, and suddenly realized how very much depended on it—especially for Penny—Swimmer hesitated. He had an awful, sinking sensation that warned him the next hour wasn't going to be any love feast, and that his presence wouldn't improve matters a bit. Unless, of course, he could come up with something positively brilliant that might help to save the situation. But what?

Before he could call up a single top-level thought, he heard another car approaching. From the familiar sound of it he knew that it was old Doc's big chauffeur-driven limousine. Swimmer, with Ripple close behind him, slipped into the cover of the nearest flower bed to give his unwilling brain a little more time. It was well that he did so.

From the moment he stepped from his car, followed by a worried Mr. Tippet, it was obvious that the great Dr. Rufus Hoffman was in a rage. He moved in thunderous silence toward Mr. Owl and Mr. Hogarth, but halfway to the table he stopped and stood glaring at them like a wrathful god.

"Blackmailer!" he rumbled ominously, pointing a quivering finger at Mr. Hogarth. "Threatening me with that devilish column of yours!"

"Right, Doctor." Mr. Hogarth nodded and smiled. "I'm a blackmailer. But it got you here."

"And you—" The quivering finger jabbed at Mr. Owl. "You confounded Cherokee Shylock!"

Mr. Owl nodded, and his black eyes crinkled. "Oh, I've often extracted a pound of flesh, Doctor, but it was always for a deserving client. Don't you feel Swimmer is very deserving?"

"He deserves nothing! I'm fed up with him, and I can do without him. Of all the unmannered, opinionated, back-talking—"

"Why—why, he's not anything of the kind!" cried Penny, who had been standing unnoticed to one side, clinging tightly to Scruff. "Swimmer's the nicest, bravest, most unselfish—"

Dr. Hoffman whirled on her and saw Scruff for the first time. "Great Jupiter!" he gasped and took a step backward. "Hang on to that beast!"

"He won't hurt you if you'll just be nice to people!" Penny snapped.

"Eh? Who are you, and what are you doing here?"

"I'm Penny Jones, and—and Swimmer's just adopted me, and I'm here because Clarence has bought the trout farm, and this is where Swimmer and I and the rest of us are going to live."

"I see." Dr. Hoffman's voice was icy. "You're that incredible paragon of childhood I've been hearing so much about. And don't tell me Swimmer's adopted you, because animals don't adopt people."

"He has, too, adopted me!" Penny told him hotly, "and if

you don't believe it, just ask Mr. Owl. And—and that's your whole trouble, you keep thinking of Swimmer as an animal when he's really more of a person. And—and you ought to be ashamed of yourself for paying that horrible Jules to catch him, 'cause—'cause that Jules tried his best to kill him, and—and—"

"What nonsense!"

"Nonsense nothing!" Penny cried. "It's the truth, 'cause I was there. That Jules and his ugly black dog chased us for miles, and if Swimmer and Scruff hadn't fought him—"

"I don't believe you!"

Penny stamped her foot. "I don't care what you believe! And I don't blame Swimmer for running away from you! Why, you're nothing but—but—"

"An old blatthead!" cried Swimmer, coming angrily from the flower bed where he'd been trying to hold his tongue. "That's what you are—a skrink and a blatthead!"

That blew it, as Swimmer realized on the instant, but by this time he didn't care. It was good to get it off his chest.

Then suddenly Clarence was having it out with Dr. Hoffman and getting it off his chest too, and so was Mr. Hogarth and even Mr. Tippet. Only Mr. Owl was quiet. He stood listening, black eyes crinkling, smiling his secret smile while the others stormed and threatened and blamed even after everything had been said twice.

Into the middle of this fracas came Ripple, shaking her head. "No!" she managed to say. "No! No!"

There was an abrupt silence. Dr. Hoffman stammered, "You—you're not Swimmer!"

Ripple took his large plump hand between her two small ones and peered up at him earnestly. "I . . . am . . . Swim-mer's . . . mate."

"You—you are Swimmer's *mate?*" Dr. Hoffman's voice

cracked on the last word and went up a full octave. "How astonishing!" he said and sank down on the grass beside her. "Why didn't someone tell me about you?"

Mr. Owl sat down on the grass with them. "Perhaps," he murmured, "it is better this way. Her name is Ripple. Isn't she wonderful?"

"Absolutely wonderful!" Dr. Hoffman agreed, and it was obvious to Swimmer that a hard hunk of ice had suddenly melted. Old Doc had really flipped.

And why shouldn't he? Swimmer thought. After all, anyone with half a grain of frog sense could see that she was cute as a water bug and bright as a chickadee. As for the rest of it, even a one-eyed newt . . .

"Clarence," said Dr. Hoffman, as he looked about approvingly. "You've bought this place, haven't you?"

"Yes, Doctor."

"Seems just right for our needs. Will you lease it?"

"Of course, Doctor."

"Then get the house in shape. Add more rooms if necessary. You'll need space for a housekeeper, and there'll be Miss Primm—and Penny here—" Dr. Hoffman paused and glanced at Penny, who suddenly smiled. "You know, redheads do have spirit!" But he scowled at Swimmer. "I'm not sure about you. Maybe, if you can learn to control that devilish tongue of yours—"

"Sure, Doc. To get what we want, we've all got to make con—con—what's the blatted word again?"

"Concessions," said Clarence. "Why don't you and Ripple go and play in the trout ponds while we take care of some business? The ponds are all yours, now."